WHISKERS IN THE WIND

An Adult's Guide to Navigating Grief After the Loss of a Beloved Pet

JCR Publishing

© *Copyright 2024. JCR Publishing*

Table of Contents

About the Author

My name is Julie. I am a devoted animal lover that recently experienced the devastating loss of three out of my five pets due to age and illnesses, all within a short period of time. This personal journey has given me deep empathy for anyone enduring the heartache of losing a beloved companion. I held a private funeral, bid them a heartfelt farewell, and laid them to rest together beneath a beautiful tree in my backyard, marking their graves with memorial stones and a sign in their honor.

Their memory lives on through photographs covering my walls, and their collars and pet tags displayed in my living room. Every time I see that tree outside, I think of them, keeping their presence close. I firmly believe that losing a pet is one of life's most devastating experiences, and though the grief can feel overwhelming and unbearable, the love and bond shared between us makes every moment of my heartache worth it. With all of this in my heart, I remain committed to adopting more pets that need homes.

Dedication

To every soul who has loved and lost a pet, this book is for you.

To those who've woken up to wagging tails and purring companions, who've shared whispered secrets with floppy ears and soft paws, who've rearranged their lives around walks, belly rubs, and mealtime rituals. To those who have known the purest kind of love, the kind that asks for nothing and gives everything in return.

This is for the ones who've held trembling paws in their final moments, whispered goodbye through tears, and felt the unbearable silence when they were gone. For the people who carry the weight of their absence like a shadow, and yet still find joy in the memories they left behind.

And to the pets—our mischievous troublemakers, loyal shadows, and gentle healers. You've taught us the meaning of unconditional love and left paw prints that will never fade.

To my own beloved companions, whose presence shaped my life in immeasurable ways, and to every reader holding their pet's memory close, may this book be a reminder: the love you shared will always remain, in every quiet moment, every wagging tail, and every whisker in the wind.

This is for you.

Introduction

Setting the Stage

The Pawprints on Our Hearts

You know that moment when you're absentmindedly reaching for the leash, only to remember there's no eager face waiting by the door? Yeah, that one. It hits you like a tidal wave. One second, you're going about your day, and the next, you're knee-deep in a flood of memories, wondering how the world can keep spinning when your furry best friend is no longer in it.

Let me guess - you've heard it all already. "It was just a pet." "You can always get another one." "At least it wasn't a person." Newsflash, folks: our pets aren't "just" anything. They're family, confidants, and sometimes the only beings who genuinely get us. And now there's an "Oscar"-shaped hole in your life that feels impossible to fill.

Here's the thing - grief doesn't come with a rulebook, and there's no "right" way to mourn your pet. Maybe you find yourself smelling and ugly-crying into one of their old, stinky, stuffed toys at 3 AM. Or perhaps you're the type who throws yourself into work, trying to outrun the pain. Guess what? Both are perfectly valid. Your journey through grief is as unique as the bond you share with your pet.

Remember when "Reggie" decided that the corner of your brand-new couch was now also his brand-new scratching post? Or that time "Lucy" got a hold of that birthday cake you had made for your son's 1st birthday and ate the entire thing? Candles and all? I bet you're smiling about all of that now. That's the beautiful paradox of grief - it transforms our deepest sorrows into cherished memories, illuminating the beauty found within our heartache.

Now, you might be wondering, "Who's this person claiming to understand what I'm going through?" Well, I'm not just the author - I'm a fellow traveler on this agonizing road of pet loss. I've felt the sting of an empty dog bed, the silence where a purr used to be, and the overall quietness in the house when you get home. And let me tell you, it's a treacherous journey that can feel lonelier than a solo hike up Mount Everest. Sadly, I've had to deal with this 3 times in the last year, and that's why I decided to write this book.

But this is where things get interesting - we are not alone. Not by a long shot. Millions of pet owners have walked this path before us, and millions more will follow. We're part of a vast, invisible community connected by love, loss, and tiny pawprints on our hearts.

This book? It's not a magic wand that'll make the pain disappear. (If I had one of those, believe me, I would have dislocated my arm by now waving it around). Instead, think of it as a trusted friend, someone who has felt the exact same pain, a shoulder to cry on, and a gentle guide all rolled into one. We're going to forge ahead together, finding our way through grief toward healing.

We'll dive into the nitty-gritty of pet loss - the stuff nobody talks about, but everyone experiences. How do you deal with the deafening silence in your home? What do you say to well-meaning but clueless friends? And how on earth do you handle finding that stray tennis ball months later?

But it's not all doom and gloom, I promise. We'll also explore ways to honor your pet's memory, find meaning in your loss, and yes, even rediscover joy. Because if there's one thing our pets would want, it's for us to be happy, right?

So, grab a cup of tea (or something stronger - no judgment here), maybe a box of tissues, and let's embark on this journey together. It won't always be easy, but remember - every step forward, no matter how small, is a step towards healing.

Ready to take that first step? Let's go! Let's do it for our "Oscars," for our "Lucy's," for our "Reggie's," and for all the other furry, feathered, or scaly friends who've left those pawprints on our hearts.

Chapter 1

The Unbreakable Bond

a. More Than Just a Pet: The Profound Human-Animal Connection

Remember the last time you walked through your front door and shoulders slumped from a day that felt like it lasted a week? There they were – tail wagging or purr rumbling, eyes shining with unconditional love. At that moment, the weight of the world just instantly seemed to lift.

Our pets aren't just animals we keep around for companionship. They're our confidants, our comfort, our constant in a world of variables. They're the ones who don't judge us for eating ice cream straight from the tub at 2 AM, who listen to our deepest fears without a whisper of judgment, and who somehow know exactly when we need a furry hug.

"But they're just animals," some might say. Oh, how wrong they are! These creatures are emotional magicians, turning our lead-heavy days into gold with nothing more than a nuzzle or a minor case of the zoomies. They're the guardians of our joy, the keepers of our secrets, and often, the glue that holds our sanity together.

Think about it – how many times has your pet been your only source of comfort after a tough day? How often have they made you laugh when you thought you'd forgotten how? They're not "just pets" – they're family members with fur (or scales or feathers).

Science backs this up, you know. Studies have shown that interacting with pets can lower blood pressure, reduce stress hormones, and even boost our oxytocin levels – that's the "love hormone," folks. In other words, our pets are literally good for our health. They're like a walking, barking (or meowing) antidepressant but have softer fur and better side effects. But it goes deeper than just the physiological benefits. Our pets see us at our worst – bed head, morning breath, ugly crying over a rom-com – and love us anyway. They don't care about our job titles, bank balances, or social media following. To them, we're simply their humans, and that's enough. They teach us about unconditional love, about living in the moment, about finding joy in the simplest things. Ever watched a dog lose their mind over a stick? Or does a cat become utterly fascinated by a piece of string? There's a lesson there about appreciating life's little pleasures.

Our pets are also master empaths. They seem to have a sixth sense for when we're feeling down, instinctively knowing when to offer a comforting paw or a gentle purr. They're there for the highs and lows, the celebrations and the heartbreaks. In many ways, they're the most constant presence in our ever-changing lives.

So no, they're not "just pets." They're our best friends, therapists, cheerleaders, and family. They're the ones who make a house feel like a home, who turn a bad day into a bearable one, and who remind us, every single day, that we are loved unconditionally, whether we decide to get out of bed and put pants on or not.

The bond between humans and animals is as old as time itself, but it's no less magical for its longevity. It's a connection that transcends words, that speaks to something primal and pure within us. It's a love that asks for nothing but gives everything.

In a world that can often feel cold and uncaring, our pets are the warm, beating hearts that remind us of the good in life. They're not just animals we keep – they're the keepers of our hearts, the guardians of our souls, the truest friends we'll ever know, and sometimes, as mentioned above, the only reason we may get out of bed some mornings.

b. Why It Hurts So Much: Understanding the Depth of Pet Loss

The silence. That's often the first thing that hits you. The absence of paws padding across the floor, the lack of a cold nose nudging your hand for attention, the missing weight at the foot of your bed. It's as if someone hit the mute button on your life, leaving you in a world that suddenly feels too quiet, too empty.

Did you ever think the silence would be this loud?

Losing a pet isn't just losing an animal – it's losing a piece of your daily life, a chunk of your routine, a part of your heart. It's the end of morning walks, of evening cuddles, of that special greeting when you come home. It's saying goodbye to a being who loved you unconditionally, who never judged you, and who was always there....no matter what type of crazy you were being that day...

The pain of pet loss can be as deep and raw as losing a human family member – and in some ways, it can hurt even more. Our pets are often our constant companions, present in our lives in a way that even our closest human relationships can't match. They're there for every meal, every Netflix binge, every lazy Sunday morning. Their lives are intertwined with ours in countless tiny ways that we don't fully appreciate until they're gone.

Science backs this up, too. Studies have shown that the grief process for pet loss is remarkably similar to that of human loss. The same areas of the brain light up, the same stress hormones are released, and the same emotional upheaval occurs. Your brain doesn't distinguish between "pet" and "person" when it comes to loss – it just knows that someone you loved is gone.

I lost my mother not long before I lost my cat and 2 of my 3 dogs. I felt ashamed and confused because I was almost as upset when I lost my pets as I was when I lost my mom. And my mom was "my person," so I had a really hard time grieving her death. So to have those same feelings when I lost my pets,.... I was ashamed. I felt guilty. I felt like my emotions weren't "the norm". Like I was being "too dramatic". Almost embarrassed to tell people how hard of a time I was having with them being gone. But now I know that every tear I shed, and every emotion I felt was completely normal. I wasn't a "nut job" after all. Well, at least not for that reason. WINK

Think about it – how many of your daily routines revolve around your pet? The morning breakfasts together, the playtime after work, that sweet little head resting on my lap as I watch my sleazy reality show PVR recordings from the night before. Now, each of these moments is a reminder of what's missing. It's like your life is full of tiny landmines of memory, waiting to explode with grief when you least expect it. Who is going to eat the crust off of my pizza now? I STILL find myself setting little bits of my food on the corner of my plate to give to them when I'm done eating. And as weird as this may sound, I hate the fact that I now have to "pre-rinse" my dishes before I put them in the dishwasher. Those cute little pink tongues did more than just give good kisses around here.

And it's not just about the routines. Pets offer a unique kind of companionship that's hard to replicate. They're our comfort, our constant source of unconditional love that we may have taken for granted when they were with us. They don't care if my greys are coming in or if I lost my job and can't buy the "good" treats anymore and had to resort to dollar store junk. They just want to be with me.

The absence of their pure, unconditional love creates a profound void in our lives. There's no one to lighten the mood with their playful antics when life feels overwhelming. No one is there to see us through major life changes. When we move to a new city, when we go through breakups, when we start new jobs. They're a constant in our world of variables, a touchstone we return to again and again. Losing them can feel like losing our anchor in the storm of life.

So, ya, it hurts. It hurts like hell. The pain you're feeling? Yup, it's real, it's valid, and it's a testament to the depth of the bond you shared. Your grief is a reflection of your love, and that love was beautiful and meaningful.

c. Your Grief is Valid: Addressing Social Stigmas Around Pet Loss

You've probably heard it before – "It was just a pet" – and felt the stab of those words right in your heart. Maybe it came from a well-meaning friend, a family member, or even a complete stranger. Whoever said it, the message was clear: your grief isn't seen as valid, and your loss isn't considered significant.

But here's the truth, plain and simple: Your loss is real, and your pain matters.

Society has a funny way of dictating how we should feel, doesn't it? There are acceptable losses and unacceptable ones, grief that's recognized and grief that's dismissed. And all too often, the loss of a pet falls into the "unacceptable" category.

But let's flip the script for a moment. Would anyone dare say "it was just a friend" about a human companion who made you smile every day? Would they dismiss the loss of someone who was there for you through thick and thin, who loved you unconditionally? Of course not. So why should it be any different for our pets? It's losing a piece of our daily routine, a part of our home, a chunk of our heart.

The stigma around pet loss grief can make an already painful experience even harder. It can leave us feeling isolated, misunderstood, and as I shared earlier, even ashamed of the depth of our feelings. You too, may start to question yourself, wondering if you were overreacting or if there's something wrong with you for feeling so devastated.

But in reality – there's nothing wrong with us. Our grief is a reflection of the love we shared with our pets, and that love was real and meaningful to us. It deserves to be honored and mourned, just like any other significant loss.

So, how do we tackle these stigmas? How do we stand up for our right to grieve?

Firstly, remember that you don't owe anyone an explanation for your feelings. Your grief is yours, and you have every right to feel it fully without apology or justification.

Secondly, surround yourself with people who understand. Seek out pet loss support groups, either in person or online. Connect with other pet owners who've been through similar experiences. Sometimes, just knowing you're not alone can make a world of difference. I joined a Facebook group for people that have lost their pets. I LOVE this group because every member understands how I feel whole-heartedly, and we support one another's feelings 100%.

I have never been married and have chosen not to have children. I have lived alone for 90% of my adult life. My pets are my everything. They are my babies, my family, my "children". Oscar was almost 19 when he passed away. 19! 19 years of having him in my life. 19 years of a routine with him. Nineteen years of him ripping through my garbage *so I would have something to do when I got home from work. (He was so thoughtful that way).* 19 years of living with a dog that could easily have been in the Guinness Book of World Records for "Longest Game of Fetch". (FYI, his best time was 7 hours straight) and 19 years of his sweet little face by my side; whether I was cooking, sleeping, watching tv, or going to the bathroom, he was always there with me. Now, he's not, and it doesn't feel right. There is now a missing piece in my life and in my heart.   And the same with Lucy. Lucy was one month shy of 15 years old when she passed away, and I have had her since she was about three months old. 14 years of the zoomies when I got home from work, 14 years of her trying to attack the TV if there were animals on the screen, 14 years of her always having to be touching me in some way whenever I was sitting or laying down. 14

years of pure laughs and happiness. Then, this past year, her dementia kicked in. It came in hot. One day, she seemed fine, and the next, all she would do was spin in circles and empty her bowels at the same time, for literally hours. Then sleep, eat, repeat. That was her new life. She constantly isolated herself, which was completely out of character for her because she always needed to be anywhere I was. She went from a super friendly sweetheart to a fire-breathing dragon almost overnight. It took me a long time to accept her diagnosis, so after one year of this, I decided it was selfish of me to allow her to have this awful quality of life and that it was time that they both went to the Rainbow Bridge together. So I sent them there…together….on the same day…at the same time. One of the worst days of my life.

Sorry, I veered off track there….

Thirdly, be an advocate for pet loss grief. When you're ready, share your story. Talk about your pet's meaning, how they enriched your life, and why their loss is significant. The more we normalize these conversations, the more we chip away at the stigma. I still sometimes find it hard to talk about them without doing the "fake cough" or the unneeded "sip of water" when I need a quick moment to contain myself to be able to finish the story without having to look at the person through my tear-filled eyes. But those fake gestures are slowly fading, and I now catch myself smiling when I talk about them.

Fourth, honor your pet and your grief in whatever way feels right to you. Have a memorial service, create a photo album, or donate to an animal charity in their name. There's no "right" way to mourn – do what brings you comfort and helps you process your loss. Myself, I created a little shrine to them in my living room. I have their pictures on the wall, a clipping of their fur in clear viles with paw-shaped ornaments tied to the top of each one, and their collars around a cute little candle holder I bought at the dollar store, and I love it. It may be a bit much for someone else's taste, but WHO CARES?! It makes ME feel better.

And finally, be patient and gentle with yourself. Grief isn't linear and doesn't operate on anyone else's timeline. Allow yourself to feel whatever you're feeling for as long as you need to feel it. I'm coming up on a year and a half now since I lost my little Reggie, and I still tear up from time to time when I sit and think about him for too long. I miss my chubby little neck warmer. Gawd, he was the cuddliest cat I think I have ever known.   So the next time someone tries to diminish your loss, stand firm in your truth. Your grief is valid. Your pain is real. Your love for your pet was – and is – profound and meaningful. And you have every right to mourn that loss in whatever way feels right to you.

Because in the end, it's not about what others think or understand. It's about honoring the bond you shared with your pet, the love you gave and received, and the impact they had on your life. That's what truly matters, and that's what deserves to be remembered and celebrated. They mattered, your relationship mattered, and your grief matters, too.

Key Takeaways:

1. The human-animal bond is a profound, life-changing connection that goes far beyond simple pet ownership. Our pets become integral parts of our lives, offering unconditional love, emotional support, and companionship that can significantly impact our mental and physical well-being.

2. The pain of losing a pet can be as intense and deep as losing a human family member. This grief is rooted in the daily presence pets have in our lives and the unique, judgment-

free love they offer. The silence and emptiness left behind can be overwhelming, affecting every aspect of our routine and emotional landscape.

3. Society often undervalues pet loss grief, but it's crucial to recognize that this grief is entirely valid and deserving of acknowledgment. The stigma surrounding pet loss can compound the pain, making it essential to seek support from those who understand and to honor your grief in whatever way feels right for you.

4. Scientific research supports the depth of the human-animal bond and the significant impact of pet loss, showing that our brains process this grief similarly to human loss. This validates the intense emotions many experience when losing a pet.

5. Coping with pet loss involves acknowledging the significance of your pet in your life, allowing yourself to grieve without judgment, and finding ways to honor their memory. Remember, there's no "right" way to do it – your process is unique, personal, and valid, regardless of others' opinions.

Chapter 2

The First Wave: Immediate Aftermath

a. The Shock of Loss: Coping with Sudden Emptiness

As we step from the realm of understanding our bond into the harsh reality of loss, the world suddenly feels off-kilter. It's as if someone hit the pause button on your life but forgot to tell the rest of the world to stop spinning.

The silence. Oh, the deafening silence. It creeps into every corner of your home, filling spaces once occupied by the pitter-patter of their little toe beans, the sweet sound of their meow, or the muffled bark and flapping jowls of a great dog dream.

Have you ever reached for their food bowl, forgetting they're no longer there? That moment when muscle memory betrays you, and reality comes crashing down all over again. The absence of your fur baby creates a void so tangible you could almost touch it. Their favorite spot on the couch is suddenly empty. The leash hanging by the door was unused. The travel crate in the front hall closet takes up WAY too much space, but you can't find it in yourself to move it to the basement quite yet. Each sight is a painful reminder of what's been lost.

In these raw, early moments, the world might seem surreal. Colors are less vibrant and sounds muffled, as if you're moving through life wrapped in cotton wool. This numbness? It's your mind's way of protecting you, a temporary buffer against the full force of grief. Don't fight it – it's okay to not be okay right now.

You might find yourself going through the motions – reaching for the treats at their usual snack time, calling their name when you get home. These instinctive actions aren't signs of forgetting; they're testaments to how deeply ingrained your pet was in your daily life.

So, what can you do in these first brutal hours and days? First, breathe. Just breathe. It sounds simple, but we often forget this basic act in times of deep stress. Take deep, grounding breaths. Feel your feet on the floor. Remind yourself that you're still here, still standing, even if it feels like your world has stopped.

Next, allow yourself to feel. Let your emotions flow freely. There's no "right" way to do it. Expressing your pain and heartache is healthy. Don't let anyone tell you to "get over it" or that "it was just a pet." Your loss is real, and your grief is justified. Obviously, those people are not animal owners and just don't get it.

Reach out to someone who really understands. Whether it's a friend who's been through pet loss, a family member who loved your pet too, or joining an online support group like I did on Facebook – don't isolate yourself. Sharing your pain can lighten the load, even if just a little. It helped me feel less alone with my overwhelming sadness. I realized that others were experiencing it, too, as often and as intensely as I was. Knowing that my way of grieving wasn't an overly long or excessive process compared to others made me feel a lot better.

Remember, in these early days, self-care is crucial, too. Eat, even if you don't feel like it. Rest, even if sleep eludes you. Be gentle with yourself. You're navigating one of life's toughest journeys, and taking it one breath, one moment at a time is okay. The initial shock of loss is like a tidal wave – it knocks you off your feet and leaves you gasping for air. It exhausts you. I never knew that my body was so tired until I finally layed down on the sofa and closed my eyes for 2 minutes. Then, those 2 minutes turned into one of the longest naps I had ever had. And trust me, this girl can sleep!

For now, though, it's okay to not be okay. One day at a time, one memory at a time, one breath at a time. Your pet's love will light the way, even in the darkest moments.

b. Making Difficult Decisions: End-of-Life Care and Euthanasia

There's a crossroads in pet ownership that nobody wants to reach, a decision point that feels like walking down a road you hoped you'd never have to take. End-of-life care and euthanasia – even the words feel heavy, don't they? They sit in your chest like a weight, pressing down with the gravity of their meaning.

My depth of pet loss was also compounded by the fact that I was responsible for making all 3 of their end-of-life decisions. This led me to feelings of guilt, anger, and doubt, wondering if I did the right thing or if I could have done more. Or maybe it was too soon? Or did I wait too long? Should I get a second opinion? It's a unique kind of pain, being the one to decide when it's time to end the life of someone else. Was I being selfish because I knew I would miss the way my cat made me laugh? He'd spend what seemed like half an hour trying to cover up his Reece's feces, only to strut out of the litter box like a celebrity, with nothing covered at all. Or would I miss the adorable look on my dog's face when I tell them about my day, and I actually think they were listening and understood what I had just said?... Yes, But that also didn't make the decision any easier. Now that their physical presence is truly gone, it feels like a phantom limb, an absence I can almost touch.

If you're facing this decision, my heart goes out to you. This is, without a doubt, one of the hardest parts of loving a pet. It's the ultimate act of love, but it feels like the cruelest twist of fate. How do you decide when it's time to say goodbye? How do you know if you're making the right choice?

First, let's acknowledge something important: it's okay to feel conflicted. It's normal to feel angry – at the situation, at the unfairness of life, maybe even at yourself. And guilt? That's part of the package, too. These emotions don't make you a bad pet owner. They make you a compassionate human being. When considering end-of-life care or euthanasia, it's crucial to focus on the quality of life. Are they still enjoying their favorite activities? Are they in pain that can't be managed? Are they having more bad days than good? These are hard questions to think about, but they're important ones to ask yourself. Like I said earlier, I had to do this, and now, looking back, there is absolutely no doubt that I had made the right call. I'd rather do it a day too early than a day too late.

Remember, you know your pet better than anyone. You've been their bestie, their caregiver, their friend. Trust your instincts. If you're unsure, talk to your vet. They can provide medical insights and help you weigh the options.

Choosing euthanasia, when it's the right choice, is an act of profound compassion. It's a final gift of kindness to a pet that has given you everything. It's saying, "I love you enough to put your peace above my pain." It's hard. It hurts. But sometimes, it's the most loving thing we can do.

If you're preparing for euthanasia, consider how you want to spend your pet's final days or hours. Maybe it's a day in the park, a feast of their favorite foods, or simply quiet time together at home. Create moments that you'll cherish, even though the pain. With my dogs, they were both very old and ill, but still had great appetites, so the last 2 days before they went to the rainbow bridge together, I let them feast on anything and everything. They had chili and garlic toast, meat lovers pizzas, rainbow sherbert, chocolate chip cookies, chocolate covered peanuts, kongs with peanut butter, a ridiculous amount of milkbones, chicken fingers with honey garlic sauce, Tim

Bits, potato wedges and a whole lot of canned dog food (which was a treat in my home). They both vomited the night before the appointment. It was perfect. What would a dog want more than anything on their last days? Spending time with family and eating unlimited people's food to the point of purging, then immediately going back in for more. What a great "last supper". They loved it.

I understand this may not appeal to everyone, so you can find comfort in other things like creating rituals. Write a goodbye letter to your pet, telling them all the things you want them to know. Make a paw print keepsake. Take photos, even if it feels hard at the moment – you may treasure them later. I snuggled the heck out of those guys the night before and took an "over the top" amount of selfies with them.

During the procedure itself, (I understand it's one of the hardest things you will ever have to do, but I personally think that you need to do it), you need to be there to hold them as they cross over. They shouldn't be alone. I was a blubbering mess, but the vets and vet techs get it. They may even cry with you. After my appointment, my vet walked me out the back door so I didn't have to walk past the other clients in the waiting room. Here's me, with a red, swollen face, bawling uncontrollably, and wiping my nose with the arm of my new coat. Gross. I did NOT want anyone to see that. Thank goodness that they were very considerate about that when I was leaving.

In the aftermath, be gentle with yourself. You've made an incredibly difficult decision out of love. It's normal to second-guess yourself, to wonder if you did the right thing. But try to remember – you made the best decision you could with the information you had, out of love for your pet.

You gave your pet a lifetime of love and care. Now, in these final moments, you're giving them the ultimate gift – peace. It's okay to grieve, to hurt, to feel lost. But know this – your pet's love for you was unconditional, and it remains undiminished, even in their passing. Hold onto that love. Let it be your comfort, your strength, your guiding light as you navigate the days ahead.

c. The Guilt Trip: Navigating Complex Emotions After Pet Loss

Guilt is the ghost that haunts even the most loving pet owners. It creeps in during quiet moments, whispers doubt in the dark of night, and casts a shadow over cherished memories. If you're feeling guilty after losing your pet, know this – you're not alone, and you're not a bad pet owner. You're human, and you love deeply.

Grief is not a straight path—it's a winding road filled with potholes of 'what-ifs.' Do you keep replaying those final moments, wondering if there was more you could've done? Maybe you're questioning past decisions, second-guessing choices made months or even years ago. Perhaps you're feeling guilty for feeling relieved if your pet had a long illness.

Here's a truth bomb for you: guilt is often the flip side of love. It's our heart's way of trying to make sense of a loss that feels senseless. It's the mind's attempt to find control in a situation where we ultimately had none. But guilt, while natural, shouldn't be the legacy of your relationship with your pet.

Let's tackle some common guilt trips, shall we?

"I should have noticed sooner." Hindsight is 20/20, my friend. Pets, especially older ones, are masters at hiding pain. You acted on the information you had at the time, with your pet's best interests at heart.

"I should have done more." More tests? More treatments? Remember, quantity of life isn't the same as quality of life. You gave your pet a life filled with love – that's what matters most.

"I feel guilty for being relieved." If your pet had a long illness, feeling relief at the end of their suffering doesn't negate your love. It's a natural, compassionate response.

Now, how do we navigate these turbulent emotional waters? First, acknowledge your feelings. Guilt, like all emotions, needs to be felt to be processed. But don't let it take up permanent residence in your heart.

Try this: For every guilty thought, counter it with a positive memory. "I should have done more" becomes "I gave them a life filled with love and joy." This isn't about dismissing your feelings but about balancing them with the fuller picture of your relationship.

Write a letter to your pet. Pour out your guilt, your regrets, your love. Then, write a letter from your pet to you. What would they say? Chances are, it's full of love and gratitude, not blame.

Or again, talk to someone who gets it. Connect with others who understand this unique form of loss. Sharing these mutual feelings can help lift the weight. It really helped me.

Your pet's life was so much bigger than their final days or moments. They had a lifetime of love, care, and happiness because of you. Focus on the joy you shared, the comfort you gave, the love that flowed both ways.

Guilt often comes from a place of deep love and a desire to have done everything perfectly. But perfect love doesn't exist; real love does. And real love is messy, imperfect, and sometimes painful, but it's also beautiful, meaningful, and long-lasting."

Your pet didn't need you to be perfect. They needed you to love them, care for them, and be their advocate. And you did that every single day, in countless ways, both big and small.

Your pet loved you unconditionally and wouldn't want guilt to define their legacy. Honor them by cherishing the love, joy, and happy moments you shared. Focus on the bond you had, not the what-ifs. You were a devoted pet parent, providing a life filled with happiness. Remember that love and care are what truly matters and what your pet would want you to hold onto.

Key Takeaways:

1. The immediate aftermath of pet loss can be overwhelming, characterized by shock and a profound sense of emptiness. It's crucial to allow yourself to feel these emotions without judgment and to practice self-care during this difficult time.

2. Making end-of-life decisions for pets is one of the most challenging aspects of pet ownership. When considering euthanasia, focus on your pet's quality of life and remember that it can be a final act of love and compassion.

3. Guilt is a common and complex emotion following pet loss. It's important to recognize these feelings as a natural part of grief, but not let them overshadow the love and care you provided throughout your pet's life.

4. Coping strategies such as creating rituals, writing letters, and seeking support from others who understand can be helpful in processing grief and guilt.

5. Remember that your pet's life was filled with love because of you. Focus on the positive memories and the joy you shared, rather than dwelling on 'what-ifs'. Your love for your pet, and theirs for you, continues even after they're gone.

Chapter 3

Understanding Pet Loss Grief

a. The Stages of Grief: Do They Apply to Pet Loss?

As we navigate the path of pet loss, we often grasp for something solid to hold onto. Enter the famous stages of grief: denial, anger, bargaining, depression, and acceptance. You've probably heard of them, maybe even tried to fit your own experience into their neat little boxes. But here's the million-dollar question: do they really apply when what you've lost is your furry best friend?

Grief, as it turns out, isn't a one-size-fits-all t-shirt. It's more like a custom-made suit, tailored to fit each person's uniqueness. Sure, these stages can offer a roadmap of sorts, but treating them like a checklist? That's about as useful as a screen door on a submarine.

Let's break it down:

Denial: "This can't be happening. Maybe the vet made a mistake." Sound familiar? Denial often shows up as that initial shock, the brain's way of hitting the pause button on reality.

Anger: Have you found yourself raging at the unfairness of it all? Maybe you're mad at the illness that took your pet, or even at yourself for not being able to prevent it. Anger is grief's way of saying, "This hurts, and I don't know how to handle it."

Bargaining: This is the "what if" stage. What if I had noticed sooner? What if we had tried that other treatment? It's the mind's attempt to rewrite a story that's already been written.

Depression: The heavy blanket of sadness that seems to cover everything. It is the silent, reflective side of grief, but it hits just as hard.

Acceptance: This doesn't mean you're "over it." It's more about learning to live again with the loss, and finding a new normal in a world without your pet.

Moreover, pet loss often comes with additional layers of complexity. Maybe you had to make the heart-wrenching decision to euthanize. Perhaps you're dealing with people who don't understand the depth of your loss. These factors can add extra dimensions to your grief that the traditional stages don't fully capture.

So, do the stages of grief apply to pet loss? Yes and no. They can provide a framework for understanding some of the emotions you might experience. But they're not a roadmap you have to follow, nor a checklist you need to complete.

Your grief journey is uniquely yours. Some days, you might feel like you're making progress, only to be blindsided by a wave of sadness because you unknowingly tapped the sofa with your hand after you sat down to get them to come and sit with you and remembered that they aren't there anymore. That's okay. Grief isn't about moving through stages in a specific order – it's about learning to integrate your loss into your life, about finding ways to honor the memory of your pet while slowly healing your heart.

Your pet's love for you was one-of-a-kind and genuine. It's only natural that your sorrow would be just as personal. So, take what resonates with you from these stages, discard what doesn't, and most importantly, be kind to yourself as you navigate this healing journey.

b. Grief Isn't Linear: The Emotional Rollercoaster

Imagine, for a moment, that grief is a rollercoaster. Not one of those gentle, predictable rides that go round and round. No, we're talking about a wild, unpredictable beast of a coaster, with unexpected drops, sharp turns, and moments where you feel like you're hanging upside down, unsure which way is up. One minute, you're making coffee; the next, you're crumbling while staring at their photographs. One day, you might wake up feeling almost normal, only to be blindsided by a tidal wave of sorrow when you fill your cereal bowl and then realize you don't need to fill their food bowl, too. It's chaotic, it's messy, and yes, it's entirely normal.

This erratic pattern of emotions can be overwhelming. You might find yourself thinking, "I was doing so well yesterday. Why am I falling apart today?" Well, grief doesn't move in a straight line like we would hope. It's more like a tangled ball of Christmas lights, looping back on itself, knotting up in unexpected places.

So ya, You might experience - Sudden mood swings: Happy one moment, tearful the next. Conflicting emotions: Relief that your pet's suffering is over, coupled with guilt for feeling relieved. Unexpected triggers: A dog barking in the distance, the jingle of a collar, or even a certain time of day can set off a cascade of emotions. Periods of numbness followed by intense feelings: This is your mind's way of processing grief in manageable chunks.

I feel like it's an emotional game of whack-a-mole but with no prize. Just when you think you've got a handle on one feeling, another pops up to challenge you. I hate that game now.

So, how do you navigate this unpredictable terrain?

First, accept that this rollercoaster ride is part of the process. Fighting against it only adds to your stress. Instead, try to ride the waves. When a strong emotion hits, acknowledge it. "I'm feeling angry right now, and that's okay." Or "This sadness is really intense, but I know it will pass."

Perhaps create a grief journal. Writing down your feelings might help you make sense of them and track your journey. You might notice patterns over time, like certain triggers or times of day when your grief feels more intense. Then maybe you can prepare yourself for it.

Be kind to yourself on the bad days. It's okay to cancel plans, stay in bed a little longer, and cry into your pet's favorite blanket. These aren't setbacks; they're part of what you need to do for yourself to get you through it.

Equally, allow yourself to enjoy the good moments without guilt. Laughing at a funny memory of your pet or having a day where you don't cry doesn't mean you're forgetting them or that your love was any less real.

Remember, you don't move smoothly from "devastated" to "okay". It's more like a barn dance – two steps forward, one step back, a spin, a dip, and sometimes, if you are anything like me, tripping over your own feet. But with each step, you're moving through it no matter the direction. Don't be afraid to reach out for a helping hand when the song speeds up.

 And here's a comforting thought: this rollercoaster does eventually slow down. The drops become less steep, and the turns become less frequent and sharp. You'll never forget or stop missing your pet, but you'll learn to think of them with more peace and less pain.

So buckle up, my friend. This phase is tough, but you're tougher. You'll find a new normal, and You will. Eventually, you'll smile because they will always be a beautiful part of your life story.

c. Physical Symptoms of Grief: It's Not Just in Your Head

When we talk about grief, we often focus on the emotional toll – the sadness, the anger, the loneliness. But grief isn't just a state of mind; it's a full-body experience. Your body mourns just as much as your heart does, and understanding this physical dimension of loss can be crucial in navigating your healing journey.

Maybe you feel it like a weight on your chest, a tiredness that sleep doesn't fix, or a knot in your stomach that never seems to loosen. Perhaps you've noticed changes in your appetite, sleep patterns, or energy levels. Have you ever caught yourself unknowingly staring off into space, smiling, and just thinking about all of the things they did that made you laugh? For my guys, it was how Reggie always came flying down the hall to the living room at Mach 1 speed after every quality visit to the litter box. Or how Lucy would automatically get the zoomies if I gave her a little slap with my pajama bottoms when I pulled them out of the dresser to put them on at night. Or how Oscar would sneeze over and over again by the door instead of barking when he needed to go out for a pee. Oh, how I miss those things. I find myself doing this ALL of the time. So if you think you are the only one....You're not.

These physical manifestations of grief are incredibly common, yet often overlooked or misunderstood. Let's break down what's really happening in your body when you're grieving:

1. **Fatigue:** Grief is exhausting work. Your body is processing a major life change, and that takes energy. It's normal to feel tired, even if you're sleeping more than usual.

2. **Sleep disturbances:** You might find yourself sleeping too much or too little. Insomnia is common, as is vivid dreaming about your pet. For example, I kept dreaming about being out somewhere with my pets and losing them. I guess I'm dreaming of losing them because I really did lose them but in a different way. That's what I think, anyway.

3. **Changes in appetite:** Some people lose their appetite entirely, while others find comfort in food. Both are normal responses.

4. **Muscle tension and pain:** Grief often manifests as physical tension, particularly in the neck, shoulders, and back.

5. **Digestive issues:** That knot in your stomach isn't just a figure of speech. Grief can cause real digestive discomfort.

6. **Weakened immune system:** The stress of grief can temporarily compromise your immune defenses, making you more susceptible to illness.

7. **"Broken heart" syndrome:** In some cases, intense grief can cause heart palpitations or chest pain.

But why does this happen? It all comes down to stress. Grief activates your body's stress response, flooding your system with hormones like cortisol and adrenaline. While this response is designed to help you cope with immediate threats, prolonged activation can take a toll on your physical health.

So, what can you do to manage these physical symptoms?

1. **Gentle exercise:** Even a short walk can help release tension and boost your mood. Your pet loves walks – maybe take one in their memory.

2. **Breathing exercises:** Deep, mindful breathing can calm your nervous system. Try box breathing: inhale for 4 counts, hold for 4, exhale for 4, hold for 4, and repeat.

3. **Adequate rest:** Even if sleep is difficult, try to maintain a consistent sleep schedule. Create a bedtime ritual to signal to your body it's time to rest.

4. **Nourish your body:** Eat regular, balanced meals, even if you don't feel hungry. Stay hydrated. Your pet would want you to take care of yourself.

5. **Physical comfort:** Use heat packs for muscle tension, take warm baths, or get a massage if possible. Use up those employee health benefits if you got'em!

6. **Journaling:** Writing about your physical symptoms alongside your emotions can help you process your grief more holistically if you are that type of person.

7. **Mind-body practices:** Yoga, tai chi, or meditation can help reconnect your mind and body in healing ways. I tried Yoga, but all it did was make me realize that I hate yoga. But it might be great for you! To each their own.

Experiencing physical symptoms doesn't mean you're weak or handling grief "wrong." It means you're human, and you love deeply. Your body is simply processing an enormous change, just as your heart and mind are.

If your physical symptoms are severe or prolonged, don't hesitate to consult a healthcare professional. Sometimes, grief can unmask or exacerbate underlying health conditions that need attention. I kept a journal of everything I was feeling and talked to my doctor about it. I won't go into great details here, but I'm glad I did it.

As you navigate this physical aspect of grief, be patient with your body. It's doing the best it can to support you through this. Since your pet loved you unconditionally, in sickness and in health, don't you think it's time to extend that same unconditional love to yourself?

Key Takeaways:

1. Grief doesn't follow a predictable pattern. While the traditional stages of grief can provide a framework, pet loss grief often jumps between emotions unpredictably. Your unique journey is valid, regardless of how it aligns with these stages.

2. The emotional rollercoaster of pet grief is normal. Expect sudden mood swings, conflicting emotions, and unexpected triggers. Embrace the ups and downs as part of the healing process, and be kind to yourself through it all.

3. Grief manifests physically as well as emotionally. Expect those common physical symptoms like fatigue, sleep disturbances, changes in appetite, and/or muscle tension. These are normal stress responses to loss.

4. Self-care is crucial during the grieving process. Gentle exercise, proper nutrition, adequate rest, and stress-reduction techniques can help manage both the emotional and physical symptoms of grief. I wish I had paid more attention to this one when I was at my worst.

5. There's no timeline for grief. Healing isn't linear, and it's okay to have good days and bad days. Your love for your pet was unique, and your grief journey will be, too. Trust the process and allow yourself the time and space to heal at your own pace.

Chapter 4

The Silent Howl: How Other Pets Grieve

a. Recognizing Signs of Pet Grief

As we've journeyed through the landscape of our own grief, it's time to turn our gaze to the silent mourners padding softly through our homes. You may not be the only one missing a companion; the loss also leaves a gaping hole for other pets. While we can articulate our pain, our furry, feathered, or scaled friends express their sorrow in a language all their own.

Imagine the world through your pet's eyes for a moment. Their buddy, playmate, or perhaps even their perceived protector has suddenly vanished. No explanation, no goodbye – just an absence that they don't understand. It's a loss that can change their world just as much as it changed ours.

But how do we decipher this silent language of loss? It's not as if they can sit us down and pour out their hearts over a cup of chamomile tea. Instead, we must become detectives, attuned to the subtle shifts in their behavior and demeanor.

Have you noticed your cat staring at the door, waiting, as if their friend will come bouncing back any moment? Or perhaps your dog seems less enthusiastic about their daily walk, and is always looking back to see if their friend is coming? Is their tail hanging low instead of wagging high with joy? Have they stopped eating? Have they lost interest in playing with their favorite toys? These could be the whispers of a grieving heart.

Some common signs of pet grief include:

1. **Changes in appetite:** Just like humans, grieving pets may either avoid food or find comfort in overeating. My pet

stopped eating much and even lost interest in treats—an obvious sign that something was wrong. This was especially unusual since he was famously known in our neighborhood as the "garbage disposal" at our weekly potlucks.

2. **Lethargy:** Your once bouncy pup might become a furry lump on the couch, or your playful kitty might lose interest in their favorite feather wand. With mine, I was so busy thinking about my own sadness that I didn't realize he was laying there beside me, just as sad as I was.

3. **Clingy behavior:** Some pets might become your new shadow, following you from room to room, seeking reassurance in your presence.

4. **Withdrawal:** On the flip side, some pets might retreat into themselves, spending more time alone in quiet corners of the house.

5. **Vocalization changes:** Increased whining, meowing, or even uncharacteristic silence can be signs of a heart in distress.

6. **Sleep disturbances:** You might notice your pet sleeping more than usual or pacing restlessly at night.

7. **Searching behavior:** Pets may wander the house, nose to the ground, seemingly looking for their missing companion.

8. **Changes in bathroom habits:** Stress can lead to digestive issues or even accidents in house-trained pets.

These behaviors might remind you of your own grief symptoms, and for a good reason. The bond between animals can be just as deep and meaningful as our connections with them. Your pets aren't just reacting to a change in routine; they're mourning a genuine loss as well.

It's important to note that not all pets will show obvious signs of grief. Some may internalize their feelings, much like the stoic friend who insists they're "fine" when you know they're hurting. The absence of visible grief doesn't mean your pet isn't affected – they might just be processing in their own way.

Also, be aware that your own grief can influence your pets' behavior. Animals are incredibly attuned to our emotions, and your sadness or stress might be amplifying their own feelings of loss and confusion.

Remember, there's no "normal" when it comes to pet grief, either. Just as your journey through loss is unique, so is theirs. Some pets might bounce back relatively quickly, while others might show signs of mourning for weeks or even months.

Try to be patient and observant. Your remaining pets need your love and support now more than ever. By recognizing and acknowledging their grief too, you're taking the first step toward helping them – and yourself – heal from this shared loss.

b. Species-Specific Grief Responses

Just as each person grieves in their own way, different pets do, too. The language of loss varies not just from individual to individual, but from species to species. Each creature copes with loss in its own unique way, like leaves falling differently from the same tree.

A dog's grief is compared to a loyal friend looking for someone they've lost. Dogs often form strong bonds with their companions, and when one is gone, they might search the house, look in familiar places, or act as if they're waiting for them to return. This reflects their loyalty and deep connection. Our canine companions often wear their hearts on their furry sleeves. After all, they're pack animals, and losing a pack member can leave them feeling adrift. You might notice:

1. **Increased vocalization:** Whining, howling, or barking more than usual, as if calling out for their lost friend.

2. **Clinginess:** Suddenly becoming your furry shadow, reluctant to let you out of sight, seeking comfort in your presence.

3. **Loss of interest in activities:** That tennis ball they used to chase with gusto? It might lay untouched, a poignant reminder of playtimes past.

4. **Changes in sleep patterns:** Either sleeping more, as if trying to escape reality, or having trouble settling down, restless without their companion.

5. **Decreased appetite:** Food might suddenly seem uninteresting, and their bowl may be left full as they mourn.

Some dogs might even wait by the door or search the house, their noses to the ground, looking for their missing friend. It's a heart-wrenching sight, but remember – this behavior shows the depth of their bond and is a normal part of their grieving process.

A cat may express its sadness in quiet, solitary ways. This could involve behaviors like withdrawing from social interaction, spending more time alone, or appearing lost in thought. It suggests that a grieving cat processes emotions internally, so they may be harder to notice. Keep an eye open for:

1. **Increased neediness:** Even the most independent cat might suddenly crave more attention, seeking comfort in your lap or following you from room to room. My cat Midnight, suddenly always wanted to lay on my chest when Reggie passed away. I knew something was up because in the 8 years I've had her, she only did that when she was sick and needed to go to the vet, which was twice. And I get it. She

and Reggie were so tightly bonded for those 8 years. My heart breaks for her now when I see her laying all alone sometimes.

2. **Excessive grooming:** This self-soothing behavior might increase during times of stress, a feline version of stress-eating.

3. **Changes in vocalization:** Some cats might become more vocal, meowing plaintively, while others might fall unusually silent.

4. **Lethargy:** Your once active kitty might spend more time napping or hiding, their usual curiosity dampened by sorrow.

5. **Territory marking:** Some cats might mark their territory more frequently, trying to reestablish a sense of security in their changed world.

Birds might express their loss through silence, while rabbits may show their sorrow through stillness. Each species has its own way of saying, "I miss my friend,," so make sure you do some more research on your other pets' grieving patterns and that they are okay too.

Birds: These social creatures can experience deep bonds with their cage-mates or even with pets of other species. Signs of avian grief might include:

1. **Silence:** A usually chatty bird might become quiet, their cheerful songs replaced by mournful silence.

2. **Loss of appetite:** They might show less interest in their favorite seeds or fruits, food losing its appeal in the face of loss.

3. **Decreased preening:** Grieving birds might neglect their usually meticulous grooming, their feathers becoming ruffled and unkempt.

4. **Changes in posture:** Hunched shoulders or drooping wings can indicate a bird's distress; their body language speaks volumes.

Rabbits: These gentle souls form strong bonds and can be deeply affected by loss. Look for:

1. **Decreased activity:** A grieving bunny might become less playful, their usual hops and binkies replaced by stillness.

2. **Changes in eating habits:** They might eat less or stop eating certain foods, and their appetite is diminished by sorrow.

3. **Aggression:** Some rabbits might display uncharacteristic aggression when grieving, lashing out in their confusion and pain.

Small animals (hamsters, gerbils, guinea pigs): Even these tiny friends can experience loss. Watch for:

1. **Lethargy:** Less running on the wheel or exploring their habitat, their usual curiosity dampened.

2. **Changes in sleep patterns:** Sleeping more or at unusual times, their routine disrupted by grief.

3. **Decreased appetite:** Less interest in food or treats; even their favorites might go untouched.

4. **Hiding:** Spending more time in their sleeping area, seeking solace in dark, quiet spaces.

It's okay if you're unsure—pets can surprise us with the depth of their emotions. You know your pet best, and any significant change in their behavior following the loss of an animal companion could be a sign of grief.

Remember, just like humans, not all pets will display obvious signs of mourning. Some might seem relatively unaffected, while others might grieve deeply. Neither response is "wrong" – it's simply their individual way of processing the change in their environment.

As you observe your surviving pets, be patient and compassionate. They're navigating a confusing and emotional time, much like you are. Let's explore ways you can help your pets cope with their loss through understanding and support.

c. Helping Your Surviving Pets Cope

Just as you need comfort, they need you now more than ever. Your surviving pets are looking to you for guidance, reassurance, and love as they navigate this confusing time. While you can't explain to them in words what has happened, your actions and attention can speak volumes.

Here are some practical steps you can take to help your surviving pets cope with their loss:

1. **Maintain Routine:** Pets thrive on routine, and this becomes even more crucial in times of stress. Try to keep feeding times, walks, and playtimes as consistent as possible. This predictability can provide a sense of security when their world feels off-kilter. It provides them with stability in an uncertain time.

2. **Extra Quality Time:** Spend additional time with your pets. Have you tried sitting quietly with them, offering the gentle touch they might need? Sometimes, just your presence can be incredibly comforting. This shared time can be healing for both of you, a quiet communion of shared grief and love.

I spent a lot of time talking to my surviving pet and telling him that I missed the others and that I was sure he missed them, too. When I said their names, his ears went down and he looked over at the empty dog bed where they used to lay. I swear, he understood what I was saying.

3. **Encourage Play:** While respecting their mood, try to engage your pets in play. Physical activity can help reduce stress and anxiety. It might take some coaxing, but a game of fetch or a new catnip toy might provide a welcome distraction. It can spark a moment of joy in the middle of their sadness.

4. **Provide Comfort Items:** Allow your pets access to the belongings of their departed friend. The familiar scent can be comforting, like a warm blanket on a cold day. However, if this seems to increase their distress, it's okay to gradually remove these items.

5. **Consider New Stimuli:** New toys, treats, or even rearranging their living space slightly can provide mental stimulation and help create positive associations during this difficult time. Maybe now's the time to indulge in a few extra treats—just this once. After all, a little spoiling never hurt anyone, right? He's not fat; he's "embracing his gravitational pull".

6. **Respect Their Space:** While offering comfort, it's important to allow your pets to have alone time if they seek it. Create quiet, safe spaces where they can retreat if feeling overwhelmed. Sometimes, we all need a little cave to hide in when the world feels too big.

7. **Maintain Your Composure:** Pets are incredibly attuned to our emotions. While it's natural and healthy for you to grieve, try to remain calm around your pets. Your steady

presence can help them feel secure during this difficult transition.

8. **Consider Pheromone Products:** Products mimicking calming pheromones can help reduce stress for cats and dogs. Consult with your vet about options like Feliway for cats or Adaptil for dogs. Think of these as gentle, invisible cuddles for your pet.

9. **Gradual Changes:** If you need to make changes to your pet's routine or environment, do so gradually. This might include things like moving food bowls or litter boxes that were shared with the deceased pet. Small steps make for an easier journey.

10. **One-on-One Attention:** If you have multiple surviving pets, make sure to spend individual time with each of them. This can help prevent feelings of competition for your attention. Each pet should feel like the star of their own show.

11. **Consider Professional Help:** If your pet's grief seems prolonged or severe, don't hesitate to consult with your veterinarian. They can offer additional strategies or even recommend pet bereavement counselors. Sometimes, we all need a little expert guidance. I didn't even know these existed until I was researching about pets grieving.

12. **Patience and Understanding:** Above all, be patient. Just like human grief, pet grief isn't linear. There may be good days and bad days. Your understanding and consistent love will be their life raft during this storm.

Remember, helping your surviving pets cope isn't just about alleviating their distress – it's also an opportunity for you to bond more deeply. Grieving together can forge an even stronger connection between you and your pets. As you comfort them, you might find comfort in return.

As you go through this together, be open to the healing power of your bond with your surviving pets. They may not understand the concept of death, but they understand love, comfort, and companionship. So, by being there for them, you're honoring the memory of your departed pet and reaffirming the lasting power of the human-animal bond.

In time, you may find that helping your pets through their grief becomes a source of strength and healing for you as well. After all, the love we share with our pets – both those we've lost and those still with us – is a testament to the power of companionship, even in the face of loss.

Key Takeaways:

1. Silent Mourners: Our surviving pets grieve too, often in ways that mirror human grief. They may show signs like changes in appetite, sleep patterns, and behavior. Recognizing these signs is crucial in helping them cope.

2. Grief Speaks Many Languages: Different species express grief uniquely. Dogs might become clingy or vocal, cats may withdraw or mark territory, birds may fall silent, and small animals may show decreased activity. Understanding these species-specific responses helps us provide targeted support.

3. Routine as Anchor: Maintaining consistent daily routines provides a sense of security for grieving pets. Regular feeding times, walks, and play sessions offer stability amidst emotional turmoil.

4. Comfort in Togetherness: Spending extra quality time with surviving pets can be mutually healing. Your presence and

gentle touch can provide immense comfort during this difficult period.

5. Patience is Key: Pet grief, like human grief, isn't linear. Some days will be better than others. Being patient, understanding, and consistently loving helps both you and your pets navigate the journey together, potentially forging an even deeper bond through shared healing.

Chapter 5

The Ripple Effect: Pet Loss and Family Dynamics

a. When Family Members Grieve Differently

Grief doesn't come with a handbook, and even in the same family, the journey can look very different for each person. It's like your family being in a corn maze, and everyone is on a different path, but they are all trying to find the exit. You may have all taken different ways, but you all eventually get to the exit.

Have you felt alone, even while grieving together under the same roof? It's a common experience, and it can add an extra layer of complexity to an already challenging time. Some family members might retreat inward, seeking solitude to process their emotions. Others might need to talk, to share memories, to externalize their grief. And then there are those who might seem to bounce back quickly, leaving others wondering if they even cared at all.

These differences can create tension, misunderstanding, and even resentment if not addressed with care and compassion. It's crucial to remember that there's no "right" way to handle your grieving emotions. Your quiet introspection is just as valid as your sister's need to create a photo collage of your departed pet.

So, how do we navigate these emotional waters without causing more pain? Here are some strategies:

1. Acknowledge the differences: Start by openly discussing that it's okay to grieve differently. This simple acknowledgment can alleviate a lot of tension.

2. Create space for individual expression: Allow each family member to mourn in their own way. If Dad needs to be alone in the garage, let him. If your teenager wants to write poetry about the pet, encourage it.

3. Find common ground: While respecting individual grieving styles, look for ways to come together. This could be as simple as sharing a meal and allowing space for anyone who wants to share a memory.

4. Organize a family remembrance ritual: This can be a beautiful way to honor your pet while bringing everyone together. It doesn't have to be elaborate - lighting a candle, planting a tree, or creating a memory box can all serve as meaningful rituals.

5. Practice active listening: When a family member wants to talk, really listen. Try to understand their perspective without judgment or the need to "fix" their feelings.

6. Be patient: Grief isn't a race. Some family members might seem to move on quickly, while others might struggle for longer. Neither is wrong - it's just different.

7. Seek outside support if needed: Sometimes, family dynamics can be too complex to navigate alone. Don't hesitate to seek the help of a grief counselor or therapist if tensions are running high.

Your family is on this journey together, even if you're taking different paths. You can support each other through this tragedy by respecting each other's grieving styles and finding ways to connect despite the differences.

It's okay if your family's grief doesn't look picture-perfect. It's messy, it's complicated, and it's real. And in that realness, there's beauty and strength. Your shared love for your pet brought you joy in life - let it be a source of connection and healing in loss, too.

b. Helping Children Navigate Pet Loss

For a child, losing a pet might be their first encounter with death— a perplexing, painful concept that needs gentle guidance. To a child, a pet isn't just an animal—they're a playmate, a best friend, and sometimes the keeper of secrets. The loss of such a special friend can be earth-shattering for little hearts.

Have you struggled with finding the right words, wishing to shield them from pain while knowing you can't? It's a delicate balance, but remember, your honesty and support now can help shape how they deal with loss throughout their lives.

Here are some compassionate ways to help children navigate pet loss:

1. Be honest and use clear language: Avoid euphemisms like "put to sleep" or "passed away." These can be confusing for children. Instead, use simple, direct language: "Fluffy was very sick and died." It might feel harsh, but it helps children understand the permanence of death.

2. Explain death in age-appropriate terms: For younger children, you might say, "When someone dies, their body stops working. They can't eat, sleep, or play anymore." You can go into more detail about the body's functions ceasing for older kids.

3. Allow and validate their emotions: Let them know feeling sad, angry, or confused is okay. There's no "right" way to feel. You might say, "I know you're feeling really sad. I'm sad too. It's okay to cry if you need to".

4. Share your own feelings: By expressing your own grief, you show children that it's normal and okay to mourn. It also creates an opportunity for shared comfort.

5. Answer questions patiently: Children may ask the same questions repeatedly as they process the loss. Be patient and consistent in your answers.

6. Create opportunities for remembrance: Encourage children to draw pictures of their pet, write stories about their favorite memories, or create a memory box with the pet's toys or collar.

7. Read books about pet loss: There are many wonderful children's books that address pet loss. I actually wrote one of them as well. Reading these together can open up conversations and help children feel less alone in their grief. If you are interested in my book for children ages 3-12, it is called "Whiskers in the Wind: A Child Story Book and Guide to Navigating Grief After the Loss of their Furry Friend".

8. Hold a small ceremony: This can be as simple as planting a flower or burying a letter they wrote to them. It gives children a tangible way to say goodbye.

9. Be prepared for delayed reactions: Some children may not react immediately to the loss. Grief might surface days, weeks, or even months later. Stay open to conversations and watch for changes in behavior.

10. Maintain routines: While it's important to acknowledge the loss, maintaining regular routines can provide a sense of security during an emotionally turbulent time.

11. Consider including them in end-of-life decisions: If appropriate, involving children in decisions about euthanasia or burial can help them feel included and give them a sense of closure.

12. Be cautious about replacing the pet: While getting a new pet might seem like a good way to ease the pain, it's important to allow time for grieving. Discuss this as a family when everyone feels ready.

Keep in mind that children are remarkably resilient, but they also look to adults for cues on how to handle difficult situations. By approaching pet loss with honesty, compassion, and openness, you're not just helping them through this specific loss - you're equipping them with valuable emotional tools for life.

It's okay if you don't have all the answers. Sometimes, the most comforting thing you can do is simply be present, offering a listening ear and a warm hug. Your child may surprise you with their insights and their capacity for love and healing.

In the end, helping a child navigate pet loss is about more than just getting through a sad time. It's about teaching them that love persists beyond loss, that it's okay to feel deeply, and that we can find moments of beauty and connection even in sadness.

c. When Your Partner "Doesn't Get It"

Sometimes, the one person you rely on for support just doesn't understand why losing your pet hurts you so deeply. It can feel like you're speaking two different languages—To them, grief is overwhelming, and they seem detached from the emotional impact. This disconnect can lead to feelings of loneliness, resentment, and even anger, adding another layer of complexity to your grieving process.

But before we dive into strategies for bridging this emotional gap, let's take a deep breath and remember: different grieving styles don't necessarily indicate a lack of care or empathy. Your partner might be processing the loss differently, or they might not have had the same bond with your pet that you did.

So, how do we navigate this tricky terrain? Here are some compassionate approaches:

1. Share specific memories: Instead of trying to explain your grief in abstract terms, share concrete memories that illustrate your pet's importance. "Remember how Reggie always snuggled into my neck and rubbed noses with me? I miss that so much." This can help your partner understand the void you're feeling.

2. Express your needs clearly: Your partner isn't a mind reader. If you need more support, say so directly. "I'm really struggling with Reggie's absence. Could we spend some time looking at photos together?"

3. Create shared moments of remembrance: Invite your partner to participate in honoring your pet's memory, whether through a small ritual or creating a memorial together. This shared experience can foster understanding and connection.

4. Explain the impact: Sometimes, partners might not realize how deeply a pet's loss affects daily life. Share how your routines have changed: "I keep expecting to hear his collar jingling when I come home. The house feels so quiet now."

5. Seek to understand their perspective: Ask your partner about their feelings regarding the loss. Their apparent lack of grief might be masking other emotions or concerns.

6. Find a middle ground: If your partner isn't comfortable with extensive mourning, agree on a specific time or place where you can freely express your grief without judgment.

7. Seek outside support: If you need more emotional support than your partner can provide, consider joining a pet loss support group or talking to a therapist again.

8. Practice patience: Remember that empathy can be developed over time. Your openness about your feelings might gradually help your partner understand.

9. Acknowledge their support in other areas: Even if they don't fully understand your grief, your partner might be supporting you in other ways. Recognizing this can help maintain a positive connection.

10. Show vulnerability: Sometimes, allowing your partner to see your raw grief can be more powerful than any words. It's okay to cry in front of them or ask for a hug when you're feeling low.

It's not about making your partner grieve exactly as you do. It's about finding a way to both feel supported and understood in your grief while respecting their different experience of the loss.

As discussed earlier, your grief is valid, regardless of whether everyone in your life understands it. But by approaching this challenge with patience, clear communication, and a willingness to meet in the middle, you and your partner can navigate this difficult time together.

Your pet brought love and joy into your life. Let that love be the bridge that helps you and your partner connect, even in the face of loss and differing grief responses.

Key Takeaways:

1. Grief is a unique journey for each family member. Recognizing and respecting these differences is crucial for maintaining harmony during a challenging time. Create space for individual expression while finding common ground through shared rituals or activities.

2. For children, losing a pet may be their first encounter with death. Approach the topic with honesty, using clear, age-appropriate language. Encourage expression through art, storytelling, or small ceremonies to help them process their emotions.

3. When partners grieve differently, it can strain relationships. Bridge the gap by sharing specific memories, clearly expressing needs, and inviting participation in remembrance activities. Patience and open communication are key to fostering understanding.

4. Family dynamics play a significant role in the grieving process. Be prepared for unexpected reactions and delayed responses, especially in children. Maintain routines to provide a sense of security amidst emotional turmoil.

5. Seeking outside support, whether through counseling or support groups, can be beneficial when family members struggle to connect in their grief. Remember, the goal isn't

uniform grief, but mutual support and understanding during a difficult time.

Chapter 6

Honoring Your Pet's Memory

a. Creating a Memorial: Ideas for Remembrance

Honoring a pet's memory can feel like setting up a "Hall of Fame" for the one who knew your secrets, stole your socks, and forever stole your heart. A memorial isn't about making grief heavier; it's about creating a joyful tribute to all the little ways they made life better. Think of it as an award ceremony for the "Greatest Companion of All Time"—with the spotlight shining on that furry, feathery, or scaly superstar who left those pawprints on your heart.

Imagine displaying a photo of your pet in their prime "guilty" moment, like the time they proudly paraded around with your favorite shoe or a picture of them with that guilty look when you came home from work to find your new sofa ripped to shreds and the stuffing all over the place. Or maybe you'd prefer a simpler tribute: a favorite collar, tag, or blanket placed in a shadow box, preserving their presence in a small but meaningful way. Memorials don't need to be elaborate—they're about keeping the spirit of your pet alive. What object sums up their personality best? Maybe it's that slobbery tennis ball, their favorite food bowl, or even the spot on the couch that's forever "theirs."

For some, a small garden stone or plaque with their name feels right, marking a place in the yard where they loved to nap in the sun or watch the world go by. Or consider a custom piece of art that captures the sparkle in their eyes or the mischief in their smile— something that makes you laugh and cry in the same breath.

Whether it's an indoor tribute or an outdoor marker, a memorial should feel as personal as the bond you shared. If you're looking for a unique way to honor them, how about creating a "champion title" for them? Picture a framed certificate that reads "Master of Squirrel Chasing, 2024" or "Snack Begging Specialist." These little touches remind you of the quirks that made them truly irreplaceable.

A memorial isn't just a reminder of the loss; it's a celebration of all the things that made your pet special and unique. Create something that makes you smile whenever you look at it. After all, they'd want you to remember them with the same happiness they brought into your life every day.

b. Rituals and Ceremonies: Finding Closure

Planning a ceremony for a pet can feel a bit like organizing an awards show for the one who'd probably interrupt it to chase a squirrel. A memorial ritual is about creating a moment of togetherness, a way to mark their place in your heart forever. And the beauty of it? There's no right or wrong way to say goodbye.

Consider hosting a "Greatest Hits" night with family and friends, where everyone shares their funniest or most touching memories. Maybe one of your friends remembers how your pet once greeted them by rolling over, tail wagging, as if they'd been best friends for years. Or maybe there's a family story about that time your cat proudly brought in "presents" from the yard, leading to a small, harmless bit of chaos. Moments like these make for a perfect send-off, sharing laughs and tears as you celebrate everything that made them one-of-a-kind.

Some readers may prefer more traditional rituals. Consider a small gathering in a favorite spot, where you can say a few words of farewell, recite a poem, or play a song that reminds you of them. It doesn't have to be grand; it just has to feel right. It's your moment to connect, to remember, and to let go just a little—enough to ease the ache in your heart without losing the joy they brought into your life.

Whatever ceremony you choose, remember it's not about saying goodbye forever; it's about creating a moment of peace, where their memory can rest gently with you. These small acts don't just honor your pet—they help you connect to the love and joy they brought, making space for the heart to heal. Pets may leave our arms, but they'll never leave our hearts.

c. Keeping Their Memory Alive in Daily Life

Having a pet is like having a roommate with endless quirks—and when they're gone, it's as if they've left traces everywhere, like invisible pawprints in your home. Maybe they're not curling up on your lap or greeting you at the door, but somehow, you still catch glimpses of them in the corner of your eye or hear the phantom jingle of their collar. It's like they've become an honorary member of the house, even in their absence.

One way to keep their memory alive is to carry a little something that reminds you of them, like a small charm, a keychain with their picture, a collar tag, or a favorite photo tucked in your wallet can act as a comforting reminder, a touchstone for those days when their absence feels especially strong. They may not be physically there, but keeping a small reminder close can feel like having them along for the ride, wherever life takes you next.

c. Keeping Their Memory Alive in Daily Life

Sometimes, honoring a pet's memory means still including them in your routines in little ways. It could be as simple as greeting their photo each morning or setting their bowl in the same spot, even if it's just symbolic now. You might find yourself still chatting with them out loud, catching yourself halfway through, and smiling at the thought of how they'd tilt their head as if trying to understand. These small habits keep them close.

If you're someone who enjoys connecting with others, consider volunteering at a local shelter or animal rescue in their memory. Share your pet's story with the animals you meet, letting them know about the wonderful companion who came before. It's a way of giving back, of carrying forward the love and companionship they gave you. Imagine telling a scruffy shelter dog or a shy kitten about the friend you had—the best buddy who paved the way for other animals to find a caring home. It's a legacy that lives on, passed from one heart to another.

Another idea is to create a "paw print" in your life that celebrates their personality and the ways they changed you. For some, this could mean planting a small tree or garden in their honor—a place where you can watch something grow and thrive, just as your bond did. For others, it's about living out a lesson they taught you: to pause more often, appreciate a sunny day, or find joy in the simplest things. Every time you do, it's like they're there beside you, reminding you of the love and laughter they left behind.

Memories have a funny way of staying fresh if you let them. Instead of letting go, think of it as letting them in—into your routines, your thoughts, and your future. They may be gone, but the love they planted in you grows on.

Key Takeaways

The memory of a beloved pet deserves to be held close in ways that bring comfort, laughter, and a sense of peace. From playful memorials that celebrate their quirks to ceremonies that bring together friends and family, honoring a pet's memory is as unique as the love you shared. Each remembrance serves not only to keep their spirit alive but also to ease the ache of their absence.

Creating a memorial, whether a simple keepsake or a grand tribute, is about remembering them for the joy they brought. A framed photo of their most "guilty" expression or a stone marker in a sunny garden can remind you of the happiness they shared with you every day. Each item tells a story, preserving the moments and memories that made them irreplaceable.

Ceremonies and rituals, even the smallest acts, help provide closure. A "treat toast," a family "Greatest Hits" night, or a candle-lit moment can bring comfort, humor, and healing. These ceremonies aren't just farewells—they're celebrations of all the love, laughter, and companionship your pet brought into your life.

Keeping their memory alive in daily life is a way to hold onto the parts of them that are forever entwined with who you are. A favorite photo on your desk, a quiet greeting each morning, or volunteering in their honor reminds you that they'll always be a part of you. Honoring their memory doesn't mean holding onto sadness; it means carrying forward the love, kindness, and joy they taught you.

In honoring a pet, you're not just saying goodbye—you're creating a legacy that lives on in the small moments, the laughter, and the quiet spaces where their spirit can still be felt. This chapter of remembrance isn't an end; it's a way to make their love a part of you forever.

Chapter 7

The Power of Storytelling

a. Writing Your Pet's Life Story

Writing a pet's life story is like crafting an epic saga, starring the hero you never expected but can't imagine living without. You're not just creating a simple biography; you're writing the story of a legend—one who may have spent half their life napping but was still the greatest tug of war champion of all time.

Start by thinking of their most defining traits. If this were a movie, your pet would have their own theme song, something catchy that captures their quirks. Remember the time they heroically guarded you against the mysterious intruder at the door (a.k.a. the mailman), or that summer they proudly strutted around with a prized stick that was way too big for the front door? Their life story doesn't need to follow a traditional structure; think of it more like a collection of their greatest hits.

You might consider dividing their story into "chapters" of sorts. There could be "The Early Days," where you share the funny mishaps and adorable moments of their youth. Then maybe "The Golden Era," where they really came into their own, showing off their quirks, like their expertise in knowing the difference between the sound of a cheese wrapper vs the sound of other wrappers. And don't forget "The Age of Wisdom," when they began to slow down a little but still had that spark, looking at you with those knowing eyes as if they'd been here forever.

Ask yourself, *"What were their greatest achievements?"* Was your dog a Master of Squirrel Surveillance, tirelessly guarding the yard against uninvited guests? Or perhaps your cat was a Champion Shelf Knocker, silently clearing your countertops of fragile objects with a casual swat of the paw. These moments are what make them so memorable, and writing about them is like preserving a time capsule filled with all the laughter and love they brought into your life.

As you write, let the memories guide you. Remember that this is as much a healing process as it is a tribute. Don't hold back on the little details—the way their butt swayed when their tail wagged when they were extra happy or the way they used to drool when you were eating dinner. These aren't just stories; they're pieces of your heart, woven into a narrative that will be as funny and touching to read as it is to write. And who knows, maybe one day, you'll look back on this story and find yourself smiling through the tears.

b. Sharing Memories with Others

Sharing memories of a pet is a bit like swapping stories about a friend everyone secretly adored. There's that one tale you can't resist telling, even though your friends and family have probably heard it a thousand times. Maybe it's the time your dog heroically intercepted a hotdog at a barbecue, catching it mid-air as if it was a scene straight out of an action movie. Or perhaps it's the story of your cat, who used to bring home neighbors belongings as a gift no one asked for, but everyone remembers.

When it comes to sharing pet memories, the beauty is in the details and the laughter. You could host a "Pet Tales" night, where you and close friends or family gather to reminisce. Each person can share their own favorite moments with your pet, celebrating everything that made them unique. It's a lighthearted way to connect, mixing laughter and love with a shared sense of loss.

Or maybe you'd prefer a quieter approach. Next time you're with a friend who knows your pet well, bring up a funny memory in passing, like the time your dog somehow ended up falling asleep with her face in their shoe, or the day your cat decided to sit in your new cooler bag and his claws poked holes in the bottom so it always leaked. The best stories are the ones that make people smile before you even finish talking.

There's something deeply comforting in knowing that your pet made such an impression on others. These stories keep their spirit alive, not as a shadow of loss but as a joyful reminder of everything they brought to your life. My friends talk about how they think my dog was a human in their past life. They talk about a night we watched fireworks together (they didn't bother him. He actually enjoyed watching them), and I was sitting next to him on a park bench with my arm around him as we both looked up together, enjoying the show like we were two people on a date. As you share, notice how each story becomes a little easier to tell, turning grief into something you can smile through. It's like an invisible hug—a reminder that the love you shared was so real, it's become a memory you can carry forward, laughter and all.

c. Using Art and Creativity to Express Grief

Creating art in memory of a pet can be as simple as a sketch or as grand as a full-blown sculpture. Think of it as making a tribute worthy of the Renaissance, but with modern flair—something that might include a tennis ball and a few muddy paw prints. After all, no one deserves a masterpiece quite like the pet who doubled as your best friend and loyal partner in crime.

Maybe start small: a drawing of their favorite look (you know, the one—they had that "treat now, questions later" face). Or perhaps you want to get even more creative, making a comic strip of your pet's most "legendary" moments, like the time they tried to fit through the doggy door and got stuck, forgetting they'd grown a bit since puppyhood. The humor in these projects is just as therapeutic as the art itself, a reminder of all the joy they bring you.

You don't need to be an artist to make something meaningful. Even simple, heartfelt creations—a scrapbook filled with photos, a painted stone in their favorite spot in the yard—can serve as healing reminders of your time together. Ask yourself, *"What's the best way to capture that smile, that tail wag, that sparkle in their eye?"* And remember, this art is just for you; it doesn't need to be perfect or polished.

For some, creating poetry or writing a letter to their pet is a way of channeling grief into words, like a quiet conversation that helps bring peace. Let the feelings flow; there's no right or wrong way to create. And if you feel like adding a bit of humor, why not write a "wanted poster" for all the things they stole over the years—socks, hearts, maybe even the occasional unattended sandwich?

Art is a powerful way to express what's hard to say. It lets you process grief in a way that feels as personal and unique as the pet you're honoring. Each piece, whether a sketch, poem, or DIY craft, becomes a tribute that carries their spirit forward, a way to hold onto their memory without holding onto the sadness.

c. Using Art and Creativity to Express Grief

Creative expression offers a bridge between the love you shared and the emotions you're processing. For those who enjoy hands-on activities, consider crafting a small monument out of materials that remind you of your pet—a clay paw print, a wooden engraving, or even a framed piece of their collar or favorite toy. These items don't just serve as memories; they are part of a therapeutic process that helps transform your feelings of loss into something tangible, something you can hold or see that brings a comforting presence.

If you're more digitally inclined, why not create a photo montage, short video, or a digital photo frame that highlights their life? Compile snippets of everyday moments, like their playful pounces or curious head tilts, and set it to music that reminds you of them. Or no music. It's up to you. It's a beautiful way to capture the essence of your pet in motion, a moving story that's uniquely theirs. As you gather photos or videos, you may even find yourself laughing or tearing up, realizing just how many small yet priceless memories you have. This process can feel like a balm, giving you the chance to relive your best days while gently letting go.

And don't underestimate the power of everyday creativity. Even something as simple as writing "thank you" letters to your pet—detailing the silly moments and life lessons they left behind—can become a cherished ritual. You might feel silly at first, but as you start writing, you'll find that the memories and gratitude flow naturally, filling you with a sense of peace. You could even create a small "diary" where you jot down memories as they come, a place to capture fleeting moments and revisit them whenever you want to feel close to them again.

Art, whether in the form of painting, music, or writing, isn't just about creating a finished product; it's about finding new ways to keep the connection alive. The joy they brought you can live on in every brushstroke, every word, every memory you capture. Creativity allows you to move forward without leaving them behind, carrying a part of them with you in everything you create.

Key Takeaways

Storytelling has the power to heal, transform, and carry us through even the most profound losses. Telling your pet's story is a way to keep their spirit alive in your heart, celebrating everything they brought to your life. From writing their life story to sharing memories with friends or expressing grief through art, these acts of storytelling help you honor their memory in ways that bring comfort, joy, and connection.

Writing your pet's life story is a beautiful process of remembering, celebrating, and preserving the countless ways they touched your life. Each quirky moment, heroic "rescue," and wag or purr is a reminder of the bond you shared, bringing you closer to peace.

Sharing these stories with others is just as powerful. By reminiscing with friends or family, you create a space for laughter, connection, and mutual understanding. These stories aren't just memories; they're love, woven into every tale of mischief or affection.

Finally, expressing your grief through art allows you to capture the unique essence of your pet in a way that words can't always convey. Art offers a safe space for emotions, whether through creating a small memorial, writing a poem, or making a tribute that brings you closer to them in heart and memory. Through storytelling, you not only honor your pet's legacy but also create a comforting bridge between your love and your loss.

Each story, every memory, and all the art you create keeps them close, helping you to heal and reminding you that their spirit remains part of your life forever.

Chapter 8

Self-Care During Pet Loss

a. Physical Self-Care: Nutrition, Sleep, and Exercise

When grieving, self-care might feel like an abstract, distant concept—as though it's the last thing on your mind when all you want is to curl up and retreat. But taking care of your body is, in a way, taking care of your heart, especially when it's aching. Grief can drain you, leaving you feeling like you're running on fumes and barely getting by. Physical self-care is like plugging in your phone for 10 minutes before it dies; it may not recharge everything to its fullest, but it gives you some power to keep going, even if you'd rather just hibernate under a pile of blankets.

Let's start with the basics: food. When you're deep in grief, eating can feel like a chore, or worse, something you're "supposed" to do. But think of it as refueling. Maybe you're not up for a full, balanced meal, but something nourishing, like soup or fruit, can make a huge difference. Think of it this way: grabbing a real meal instead of just having cereal or leftover chips that you find in the back of the pantry isn't just for nutrition—it's like doing a little favor for yourself, a way to say, *"Hey, I know you're hurting, but you need this."*

Then, there's sleep. Losing a pet can leave you lying awake, scrolling through photos of them, or rehashing memories in your mind. And while it's comforting to revisit these moments, it doesn't exactly do wonders for your sleep schedule. Here's a suggestion: make a small bedtime ritual. Instead of reaching for your phone, try reading a few pages of a book, listening to calming music, or listening to an audible book. Give yourself permission to rest—think of it as recharging so you can tackle the next day with a little more strength. Besides, your pet would want you to take care of yourself, especially if it means you're ready to face another day with a bit more energy.

Finally, exercise. Now, I know this may sound exhausting (and who wants to go for a jog when your heart feels heavy?), but even light movement can make a difference. A short walk around the block, or even a few stretches, is enough to clear your mind and lift your spirits. Imagine it as a way of taking your pet along in spirit, showing them their favorite spots, or remembering the happy walks you shared. Exercise isn't about forcing yourself to feel better; it's about giving your body a little space to breathe, even if your heart is still processing everything.

So, in the midst of grief, give yourself the gift of nourishment, rest, and movement. Think of it as laying a foundation, a way to remind yourself that you're still here, still standing—even if today, that feels like an achievement in itself.

b. Emotional Self-Care: Allowing Yourself to Grieve

Emotional self-care isn't a one-size-fits-all deal; it's more like a buffet of feelings you didn't order but somehow ended up with anyway. Grief is a messy, unpredictable thing, like the tide— sometimes gentle, sometimes overwhelming, but always changing. And now you know the truth: it's okay to feel however you feel for as long as you need to feel it.

One of the first steps in emotional self-care is simply allowing yourself to feel, even if those feelings are all over the place. One moment, you might be looking at their favorite toy and feeling a wave of sadness, and the next, you're smiling at the memory of that time they ruined your favorite shoes but somehow got away with it. Emotions aren't neat—they're messy, and grief often brings them out in full force. And that's okay. Think of it like surfing a wave that changes without warning. Sometimes, it's gentle; other times, it's a tidal wave. Your only job is to ride it as best as you can.

It also means accepting those random bursts of tears that show up out of nowhere—maybe while you're folding laundry or seeing a pet toy still lying in the corner. Instead of fighting these moments, let them come. Emotions don't have to be controlled; they just need to be felt. Crying, laughing, even talking to their photo isn't strange. Think of it as staying connected to their spirit, letting them be a part of your day in a new way.

Above all, remember that emotional self-care is about embracing your own process. There's no map, no guide that says you need to feel a certain way or "move on" by a certain time. Letting yourself grieve means giving yourself the freedom to feel every ounce of love and loss without judgment.

c. Spiritual Self-Care: Finding Meaning in Loss

Spiritual self-care can feel a bit abstract at first. When grieving a pet, finding "meaning" might seem impossible, or perhaps unnecessary. But think of it more as giving your spirit a little room to breathe, letting yourself reconnect to the essence of your pet and the love you shared. You don't have to seek grand revelations—sometimes, spiritual self-care is as simple as sitting outside, closing your eyes, and feeling the breeze. It's about connecting with something bigger than the everyday routines and finding a sense of peace in their memory.

Consider a small ritual that makes you feel close to your pet, even if it's just stepping outside at sunset or sitting quietly with a favorite photo. These little moments are like "spiritual bookmarks," reminding you that the bond you shared is part of the larger story of your life. And there's something powerful in that: knowing that they are woven into your journey, even if they're no longer here physically. When you sit quietly with a memory or take a moment of silence in a place you love, you're creating a space where love and gratitude fill the gaps left by grief.

Some people find comfort in connecting with nature as part of their spiritual self-care, believing that nature holds echoes of those we've loved and lost. A walk through the park, a quiet moment by a river, or even the familiar path you took with your pet can bring a sense of calm and continuity. Think of it as a way of feeling their spirit in the world around you—listening to birds sing or watching leaves sway, knowing that they, too, are part of this natural cycle. Perhaps they taught you to appreciate the little things, like the sound of a squirrel in the bushes or the sunlight streaming through trees. Carry these lessons forward, letting them become part of your spiritual life.

For others, spiritual self-care may involve finding new ways to give back, and honoring their pet's memory by helping other animals. Again, volunteering at a shelter, donating supplies, or simply offering a kind word to an animal in need can feel like carrying your pet's legacy forward. When you care for others in their name, it's as if their spirit lives on in each act of kindness. Think of it as planting seeds of love and compassion in their honor, creating a ripple effect that turns your grief into something positive, something that uplifts others.

If you're someone who finds meaning in quiet reflection or meditation, consider setting aside a few moments each day to be with your thoughts and memories. Light a candle, take a few deep breaths, and simply allow yourself to exist in a space of gratitude. Your pet may not be there in the physical sense, but their spirit, their love, and all the joy they brought you live on. This gentle ritual can be a source of peace, a way to connect with their memory without holding onto sadness.

Spiritual self-care isn't about answers or revelations—it's about creating a place where you can find comfort, even in the midst of loss. As you nurture your spirit in these small, meaningful ways, you may find that grief becomes less of a weight and more of a reminder of how deeply you loved and were loved in return.

Key Takeaways

Taking care of yourself during pet loss is not about "moving on" or forcing yourself to forget; it's about nourishing your body, mind, and spirit in ways that allow you to process your grief. Self-care during this time isn't a luxury—it's a necessity, a way of treating yourself with the same kindness and compassion that your pet would have shown you.

Physical self-care gives your body the support it needs to navigate this time. Eating well, resting, and moving gently are small acts that help you stay grounded. Remember, it's okay to take things one step at a time, prioritizing the essentials and listening to your body's needs.

Emotional self-care is about allowing yourself to grieve in your own way. This might mean sharing stories, journaling, or simply letting your feelings flow without judgment. Grief isn't linear, and there's no set timeline. Your emotions may come in waves, each one bringing a little more healing. Trust in your process, knowing that every tear, every laugh, and every memory is part of your journey.

Finally, spiritual self-care lets you connect with the love that remains. Whether it's through quiet reflection, spending time in nature, or honoring your pet by helping others, spiritual self-care helps you find meaning in loss. Your pet's spirit, the joy they brought, and the lessons they taught live on, and by tending to this part of yourself, you carry their legacy forward.

Through physical, emotional, and spiritual self-care, you're not just coping with loss—you're building a foundation of resilience and love that honors your pet's memory. Each step, no matter how small, is a way of embracing both the pain of loss and the joy of having known them. In caring for yourself, you create a path forward where your pet's memory shines brightly, guiding you with love and comfort, one day at a time.

Chapter 9

Navigating Special Days and Seasons

a. Birthdays and Adoption Days

For many of us, a pet's birthday or adoption day is like a mini holiday—an excuse to shower them with extra treats, pull out the "fancy" toys, and let them revel in the glory they so clearly deserve. Celebrating these days after they're gone can be bittersweet, stirring up fond memories while highlighting their absence. But it can also be a beautiful opportunity to honor their life, to bring back some of that joy, even if it's in a different form.

Think back to the traditions you may have had. Maybe your dog had a "birthday steak," or your cat received their own plush throne (even if they preferred sitting in the box it came in). Remembering these little celebrations might feel painful at first, but it can also bring comfort. After all, these days were about joy—and joy is still something you can bring into your life, even without them physically there.

One way to mark the day is to light a candle or frame a photo in a special spot, like a mini birthday tribute. Perhaps you could even "re-create" the celebration by going for a walk down their favorite path or baking treats in their honor to give to your remaining pets or even for your neighbors' pets. Sure, it's not the same when they're not here to gobble it up themselves, but the gesture keeps their spirit alive, reminding you that their joy still has a place in your heart. You might even make a habit of sharing a story about them on their special day, like a "birthday toast" to their quirkiest moments.

Some people find comfort in doing something they know their pet would have loved. Did they have a favorite place to visit? A routine you followed every year? Take some time to revisit those spots, carrying them with you in memory. Engage with the thought of how much they would have enjoyed the day—it's a way of celebrating with them in spirit.

Most importantly, remember that honoring their birthday or adoption day isn't about moving on or feeling "better." It's about acknowledging the love you shared and giving yourself the freedom to smile, even through your tears. This day can be a reminder that they'll always hold a place in your heart, even though when they passed, a part of your heart was taken away.

b. Holidays Without Your Pet

Holidays have a way of highlighting what's missing, especially when that missing piece is a pet who brought its own brand of joyful chaos to the season. Maybe your dog was a Christmas stocking fanatic, or always opened the presents himself on Christmas Eve before you woke up in the morning. Or your cat thought the entire tree was just one giant climbing cat post and always broke the ornaments. Pets often have their own "holiday traditions"—whether it's chasing wrapping paper across the floor or waiting patiently for something to fall off of the thanksgiving dinner table. The first few holidays without them can feel empty, but there are ways to bring their memory into the season.

Consider setting up a small tribute as part of your holiday decorations. Maybe hang an ornament with their photo, or continue to hang their stocking with everyone else's on the fireplace mantle. Think of it as giving them a seat at the table or a place by the tree, a way to say, *"You're still part of this."* This simple gesture brings a sense of peace, a reminder that they're woven into your holiday traditions forever.

Remember, holidays don't have to be heavy with grief. While their absence may be felt more acutely, these times can also be filled with the same warmth and love they brought to your life. By finding small ways to include them, you keep their presence alive in a way that honors their place in your family. And maybe, just maybe, you'll find yourself smiling at a memory instead of it making you sad.

c. The First Year: Milestones and Memories

The first year after a pet's passing is often the hardest. It's filled with those "firsts" that remind you they're no longer by your side—first birthdays, first holidays, even the change of seasons can bring memories of moments you shared. It's a year of finding your way through a new normal that's going to have sudden moments of sadness but also chances to celebrate the love you had.

Keeping a journal of memories throughout the first year can be a healing practice. Try writing down a memory whenever one arises, whether it's funny, touching, or even bittersweet. Describe the moments that come to mind, the quirks and habits that made them unique. Imagine your journal as a "year of memories," a way to capture the essence of who they were and the ways they changed your life. Each entry becomes a small celebration of your bond, transforming grief into a tangible tribute you can revisit whenever you like.

You might also find comfort in creating a ritual for each season. If they loved the park, plan a visit during your first spring without them, bringing their favorite toy or a photo as a gentle tribute. In the fall, take a quiet walk to look at the leaves that have changed color or light a candle in their honor, reflecting on the warmth they brought to your life. By marking these milestones, you turn them from painful reminders into peaceful rituals, ways of holding onto their spirit as you move forward.

For some, the idea of "moving on" can feel overwhelming, especially in that first year. But navigating these milestones isn't about leaving them behind—it's about finding a new way to carry them with you. Their memory becomes a part of you. Every chew toy reminds you of a cute story. Each season reminds you of how they loved their W-A-L-K-S, no matter the weather. Each milestone is a chance to reflect on the love they brought into your life, reminding you that, while their physical presence may be gone, their impact on your life will never leave you.

As the year progresses, you may find that the grief softens, evolving into something gentler. The memories will still be there, but they may bring more smiles than tears. It's okay to feel sadness mixed with joy, to laugh at their memory one moment and miss them deeply the next. This is the journey of healing—a process that takes time, patience, and self-compassion. My own journey still isn't over.

By the end of the first year, you might discover that these "firsts" have helped you build a foundation of traditions that you can carry forward.

Key Takeaways

Navigating special days and seasons after the loss of a pet transforms into a heartfelt journey, allowing us to honor their memory. Marking birthdays and adoption days is a way to celebrate their life and the joy they brought, even in their absence. These "mini holidays" give you a moment to reflect, to smile, and honor the quirks and love that made them so special.

Holidays, too, can be a time of remembrance. Including their memory in your holiday traditions—through small gestures, a tribute, or shared stories with loved ones—helps keep their presence alive.

Finally, the first year after their passing is a time of transformation. Each milestone, each season, and each "first" without them is part of the process of healing. This year of "firsts" is about finding new ways to carry their memory forward, making room for their spirit in your daily life.

With each season, each holiday, and each anniversary, you honor their memory not as a loss, but as a lasting part of who you are.

Chapter 10

The Social Aspect of Pet Loss

a. Dealing with Insensitive Comments

When grieving a pet, we hope for compassion, understanding, and perhaps a few shared stories about the furry friend we miss. But, inevitably, we may encounter the kind of comments that leave us scratching our heads, thinking, *"Did they really just say that?"* Insensitive remarks can be like unwelcome plot twists in the story of grief—sudden and utterly baffling. And yet, as uncomfortable as they are, these comments often come from people who mean well but don't quite understand.

One of the classic lines that tends to pop up is, *"It was just a pet."* Now, imagine hearing that about a beloved companion who was there for you through every high and low, who listened without judgment, and who probably understood you better than most humans. It's like someone saying, *"It was just a dog,"* when it really was the one who knew you best. While these comments may sting, they come from a place of misunderstanding, not harm. They've obviously never had a pet before, so they will never get one.

In moments like these, it's okay to have a response ready— something that validates your feelings without feeding into the negativity. You could say, *"Maybe to you, they were just a pet, but to me, they were family."* Or you could simply nod and change the subject if you're not in the mood for explanations. After all, you don't owe anyone an in-depth lecture on why your grief is valid. Sometimes, protecting your peace means letting comments slide, knowing that their words don't lessen your bond.

It's natural to feel a little defensive when others minimize your loss, but try to remember that most people are genuinely trying to help, even if they miss the mark. If you're up for it, you might even share a funny or sweet story about your pet to help them understand why this isn't "just" a loss—it's a missing piece of your heart. Who knows, you may even get them laughing over the time your dog dove off the dock and landed on a kayaker that was passing by, or that time your cat stuck his head in the bathroom trash can, the lid popped off and got stuck around his neck, and he strutted around the house like nothing was out of the ordinary.

Ultimately, dealing with insensitive comments is about protecting yourself and remembering that grief doesn't need approval. Whether others understand it or not, your love was real, and so is your loss. Take comfort in knowing that your feelings are valid, even if others that have never had a pet, don't always know how to express their support and understanding.

b. Finding Support: Pet Loss Support Groups

Sometimes, the best people to talk to are the ones who "get it" without any explanation. Pet loss support groups can feel like a little safe haven where you can talk freely about your grief, knowing that no one will question it. Think of it as group therapy, but with more pet stories and the freedom to cry over a box of tissues that's always within reach.

Support groups offer a comforting, judgment-free zone, a place to share your stories, listen to others, and realize that your grief is part of a shared human experience. After all, everyone there has loved and lost a pet—they understand the silent heartache, the empty spaces, and the random pangs of sadness that hit out of nowhere. No one will ask in these spaces, *"Aren't you over it yet?"* They'll nod in understanding, perhaps even offering their own stories as a way of saying, *"I've been there too."*

Joining a support group might feel intimidating at first. After all, sharing your feelings in front of strangers can feel vulnerable. But remember, every person in that room (or on that Zoom call) is there for the same reason: to find understanding, comfort, and a sense of community. They've all felt the unique pain of losing a pet, and they're there to help you feel less alone. Some groups focus on sharing memories, while others offer guidance on healing. Either way, you're in the company of people who respect the depth of your loss.

Finding a group can be as simple as searching for local listings or asking around at veterinary offices, which often have resources for pet owners. Many groups meet virtually, which makes it easy to join from home, allowing you to connect with others without leaving the comfort of your space. Some people attend these groups regularly, finding a consistent source of support, while others may only need a few meetings to feel a sense of closure. There's no right or wrong way to do it; the important thing is to find what works for you.

The beauty of a support group is that it reminds you that you're not alone. Sharing stories, laughs, and even tears in a space filled with understanding can be one of the most healing parts of the journey.

c. Online Communities: Connecting in the Digital Age

In this digital age, the internet has become a comforting, round-the-clock support system for so many of us. Think of online communities as cozy, judgment-free "virtual hangouts" where you're surrounded by people who get it—no need to explain why you're still missing your pet six months later. And one of the best parts? You can connect with these people anytime, from the comfort of your couch, bed, or that cozy chair where your pet loved to snuggle up with you.

There's a wonderful, welcoming world of online spaces dedicated to pet loss, each with its own flavor and community vibe. You'll find groups on social media platforms, forums on dedicated pet loss websites, and even specialized apps. Some of these spaces are more about sharing stories—like a "Throwback Thursday" of your pet's funniest moments or a place to post pictures of their signature "look" (because every pet had that one look). Others focus on offering advice or hosting live chats where members can talk about their experiences, ask questions, and feel seen by people who understand. Imagine it as a global support group, one you can join without needing to put on pants or even brush your hair.

In these online communities, you'll find people sharing everything—from the big, heavy emotions to the quirky, sweet little memories that only pet owners understand. You might see someone posting about their cat's "stink-eye" face or their dog's hilarious obsession with squeaky toys. There's something comforting about seeing others go through the same ups and downs, celebrating the silly moments while supporting each other through the tough ones. It's like finding a corner of the internet that's filled with understanding and the unspoken love we all share for our pets. I myself, also joined a Tattoo Facebook Group that is for people that want to remember their pets. They show their pet tattoos, and then you can get some inspiration for your own…If you want to go that route.

One of the most beautiful parts of online communities is how they offer support no matter what time it is. Can't sleep at 2 a.m. because you're missing your furry friend? You can scroll through posts, comment on someone else's story, or share a memory of your own. You'd be surprised by how many people are there, ready to respond with virtual hugs, hearts, and words of comfort. In those moments, even the internet feels like a warm blanket, a place where you can feel connected to others who know exactly what you're going through.

If you're unsure where to start, consider looking for pet loss support groups on social media. These groups are often private, so you can share without worrying about everyone in your life seeing your posts. Many people find that joining a few different groups helps them find the right fit. Some groups are all about heartfelt advice and discussions, while others embrace humor, memes, and lighter-hearted ways to remember and celebrate pets. You can lurk quietly, read posts, or dive in and share your story—whatever feels right.

Online communities may be a bit unconventional when it comes to support, but they're a powerful reminder that love for our pets connects us in beautiful, unexpected ways. Finding support in these spaces can be like discovering a digital family, one that wraps around you in times of joy and sorrow alike. And sometimes, the simple act of scrolling through pictures of pets and reading stories of others' experiences can be the thing that helps you feel a little less alone.

Key Takeaways

Navigating the social aspect of pet loss can be a journey of finding understanding, kindness, and connection, even when others don't always "get it." Whether through handling well-meaning but off-the-mark comments or seeking out people who understand, there are ways to find comfort and community.

Dealing with insensitive comments can feel draining, but remember that your grief is valid, no matter what others say. With a gentle response or a change of topic, you can protect your peace while honoring the love you shared.

Support groups provide a safe, understanding environment where you can share your feelings and hear from others who know what you're going through. Joining a group can be a wonderful way to remind yourself that you're not alone, even if it's just for a few meetings or for an ongoing source of comfort.

Finally, online communities make it easier than ever to connect with people who feel the same way. These digital spaces offer 24/7 support, letting you share, read, and connect from anywhere. No matter where you are, there's a virtual family of pet lovers out there, ready to offer compassion, humor, and encouragement.

By connecting with others, in person or online, you're building a support system that helps you carry the love for your pet forward, finding comfort in the shared experiences and the kindness of those who understand.

Chapter 11

Grief and the Modern World

a. Social Media and Pet Loss: To Post or Not to Post?

Let's be honest—sharing pet loss on social media can feel like standing in the middle of Times Square with your heart on display, hoping someone will understand. You're in a delicate place, wanting to honor your pet but also feeling the vulnerability of sharing something so deeply personal. For some, posting about a pet's passing feels natural, a way of saying, *"Look, world, this soul mattered."* For others, it's a more private affair, where the last thing you want is a feed full of well-meaning comments when you're just trying to make it through the day.

Deciding whether to post isn't easy. On one hand, it can feel like a beautiful tribute. You're sharing a piece of their story, saying goodbye in a way that acknowledges their importance not just to you, but to anyone who may have "known" them through your stories or photos. It can be a way of receiving support, too. Sometimes, a simple "heart" or a short message from a friend or even a stranger can feel comforting. Other times, though, you might feel like social media is too "public" and not a good space for such a personal moment.

Ask yourself: *What do I hope to gain by sharing?* If posting a tribute would bring comfort—maybe by hearing from friends who also knew your pet, or by seeing a flood of sweet emojis that remind you that others care—then it could be a healing choice. But if the idea makes you feel more exposed than comforted, maybe it's worth considering other ways to honor them. There's no rule here, no "right" way to handle it, just what feels best to you.

If you're on the fence, you could even try something small and see how it feels. Maybe a single photo with a short caption—something like, *"In loving memory of my best friend"*—is enough. You might be surprised by how many people reach out to share their own memories, reminding you that your pet's impact was felt by others, too. But remember, whether you post a long tribute, a simple photo, or keep things private, it's all valid. This decision is about your heart, your comfort, and what will help you feel connected to their memory.

b. Digital Memorials and Virtual Candle Lighting

We're in a digital age where memorials aren't just flowers and gravestones anymore; now, they can take the form of online tributes, digital scrapbooks, and virtual candle-lighting ceremonies. Creating a digital memorial can feel a bit like building a cozy online shrine—a space dedicated to the joy, quirks, and personality that made your pet so special. It's a way of saying, *"I'll remember you here, where I can visit anytime."*

Imagine a webpage, a Facebook album, or even a small website where you upload your favorite photos and stories, a place where you and others can remember them. Some people set up entire tribute pages, like a mini museum of their pet's life, complete with captions, memories, and even "virtual candles" that friends and family can "light" by leaving a comment. It's a modern take on remembrance, a way to gather loved ones across the globe to honor a pet's legacy together.

And there are some beautiful possibilities here. You could invite friends to add their own photos or memories if they shared time with your pet. Think of it as creating an "online scrapbook" with stories like *"that time Max stole the Thanksgiving turkey"* or *"Bella's first snow adventure."* Each post and comment is a little piece of their life preserved, waiting to be revisited whenever you need a boost of joy or a reminder of all the love they brought into your life.

Some websites even offer virtual candle-lighting ceremonies, where you "light" a digital candle in honor of your pet and watch it "flicker" on the screen. It may seem simple, but that small act of lighting a candle in their name can feel like a quiet moment of connection. It's a comforting ritual that, even from afar, gives you a way to acknowledge their memory in a personal, meaningful way.

In a way, digital memorials give us a place to gather, share, and remember, without the limits of distance or time. If you're someone who likes to revisit memories or feels comfort in looking at photos, these online spaces can be a gentle reminder that they're still with you, in every memory, every story, and every shared laugh or tear.

c. Apps and Technology for Coping with Pet Loss

We live in a world where there's an app for just about everything— even for the tender moments of grief. Today, technology can offer unexpected sources of comfort, whether through memory-keeping apps, supportive communities, or even tools that help you pause and reflect. Think of these apps as small pockets of support you can carry in your pocket, like digital hand-holders for those days when the grief feels extra heavy.

There are apps designed specifically for those coping with pet loss, offering a safe space for reflection. Some apps act like journals, where you can write down memories, track your emotions, or even create a timeline of your pet's life. Imagine opening an app and seeing a reminder of their happiest moments—the day you first brought them home, their funniest habit, or their favorite place to nap. It's like carrying a scrapbook in your pocket, available anytime you need a smile or a little pick-me-up.

Then, there are apps with daily reflections or guided meditations that help you find a moment of calm. Some provide gentle reminders to pause, breathe, and reconnect with your feelings. For example, an app might prompt you to reflect on a favorite memory or to practice gratitude for the time you shared. These small reminders offer a way to bring moments of peace into your day, helping you navigate grief one day at a time.

Technology also offers unique ways to set gentle reminders for yourself. Maybe you set a monthly reminder to light a candle in their memory, or an alert for special dates, like their adoption anniversary. You could even use a mindfulness app to take a few minutes each day to breathe, relax, and think of a happy memory. Technology doesn't replace your pet or the emotions you're processing—it's just a new tool in your toolbox, there to support you.

And don't underestimate the power of a digital scrapbook. There are apps where you can store photos, videos, and even voice recordings, creating a "digital memory book" that you can revisit whenever you want. You could set up an album of your pet's greatest hits, from silly selfies with their upper lip stuck up in their gums, to those proud moments when they get so much attention every time you take them to Home Depot. Having these memories saved in one place can make it easier to share them with friends, family, or even with online support groups who understand what you're going through.

Technology isn't about replacing our memories; it's about giving us new ways to hold onto them. Whether it's a journal app where you can record your feelings, a scrapbook app that keeps your memories organized, or a gentle meditation app, these tools provide another layer of support on your journey. After all, the love you shared doesn't end—it simply finds new places to reside, even in the digital world.

And sometimes, there's something special about a simple reminder on your screen—a notification that nudges you to pause, reflect, and maybe even smile at a memory. Imagine getting a reminder that says, *"Take a moment to remember their favorite toy"* or *"Think of the way they greeted you every morning."* In those moments, it feels like a small message from them, a little digital nudge that says, *"Hey, I'm still with you."*

Apps and technology aren't magic cures for grief, of course, but they provide tools that can make the journey a bit more manageable. In the end, these resources are just another way to keep their memory close, to honor the love that remains, and to create gentle rituals that support you as you navigate this loss.

Key Takeaways

Grieving a pet in today's modern world comes with its own set of tools and choices, allowing you to remember and honor them in ways that feel right for you. Technology offers new avenues to share, connect, and reflect, giving you the flexibility to handle grief at your own pace, whether privately or within a community.

When it comes to social media, sharing a post about your pet's passing can be a way to honor them, invite support, and find a sense of closure. But there's no pressure to share if it doesn't feel right; your grief doesn't need public validation to be real. Posting or keeping things private is a personal choice, and both options can be healing in their own way.

Digital memorials allow you to create an online space dedicated to your pet's memory, where friends and family can share stories, leave virtual candles, or add their own favorite photos. These modern tributes become a place you can visit anytime, offering comfort and a sense of connection to their memory whenever you need it most.

And for those who find support in apps and technology, there are resources out there designed to help you navigate grief through journaling, memory-keeping, and connecting with others. Whether it's a mood tracker, a meditation app, or a digital scrapbook, these tools offer small ways to carry their memory with you, helping to make grief feel just a little lighter.

In the end, grieving a pet is a deeply personal journey, one that technology can enhance by offering new ways to hold onto the love you shared. Each post, every digital candle, and every memory saved is a reminder that their spirit is always with you, a comforting presence that remains, even as life continues forward. Through social media, digital memorials, and thoughtful apps, the love and memories live on, timeless and always within reach.

Chapter 12

When Grief Gets Complicated

a. Recognizing Signs of Depression

Sometimes, grief settles in as a quiet but heavy weight that doesn't seem to lift, like a dark cloud hanging around even on sunny days. Losing a pet can bring a unique kind of sadness, but when that sadness starts feeling more constant or overwhelming, it's worth paying attention. Think of it like this: grief is normal, but if it starts to feel like your world has dimmed, you might be dealing with something more than just sadness. This could be the beginning of depression, and recognizing it is the first step toward feeling better.

Depression can show up in sneaky ways. Maybe you're finding it harder to enjoy things that used to make you happy, or you feel like getting out of bed takes twice the effort it used to. Are you having days when even the simplest tasks feel like they take too much energy? That's one of those subtle signs that grief may be shifting into depression. It's like your body and mind are moving through thick fog, making everything feel just a little (or a lot) harder than it used to.

It's also possible to feel numb, like the colors of the world have faded. Perhaps you find yourself going through the motions, but there's no real connection or joy in what you're doing. This isn't just a rough patch—it's your mind's way of signaling that it might need a little extra care. Sometimes, even the people around you might notice a change, like you're "not quite yourself." They may mention you seem distant or withdrawn, which can be a cue to check in with yourself.

Now, it's important to say that noticing these signs isn't about diagnosing yourself or feeling like something's wrong. Instead, it's about recognizing when grief becomes heavier than it needs to be. Think of it as giving yourself permission to take a step back, breathe, and consider what you need to feel like yourself again. You might be surprised at how much of a relief it can be to acknowledge those feelings and start taking steps, even small ones, toward feeling better.

If any of this sounds familiar, it might be time to think about self-care with a bit more intention. Little things, like going outside for fresh air, calling a friend, or even allowing yourself a good cry, can help lift some of that weight. But if the heaviness persists, know that reaching out for support—whether from loved ones or a professional—can make a world of difference. Remember, depression doesn't mean you're weak; it just means you've been carrying a lot, and there's no shame in getting a bit of help to lighten that load.

b. Anxiety and PTSD After Pet Loss

Losing a pet can shake up your sense of security, sometimes in ways that surprise you. Maybe it's a feeling of anxiety that creeps in or even moments of panic that you can't quite explain. For some people, especially if the loss was sudden or traumatic, the emotions can be more intense, sometimes bordering on what's known as PTSD. It's like your mind is stuck in "alert mode," unable to fully relax, as if you're waiting for something else to happen.

Anxiety after pet loss might show up as a constant worry or a lingering sense of unease. You might find yourself feeling jumpy or tense, with physical signs like a racing heart or tightness in your chest. If you're struggling to shake off nervous energy, or if certain places or activities trigger a sense of dread, it could be a sign that your grief has a layer of anxiety mixed in. It's as if your brain is holding onto the loss, replaying it in ways that can make it hard to fully process.

PTSD can bring a different set of challenges. For example, you may find yourself avoiding certain places—like the park you used to visit together or the vet's office—because they bring back too many painful memories. Or you may even experience flashbacks, moments when a memory feels so vivid that it's like you're reliving it. It's a disorienting experience, and it can make it feel as though the grief is fresh all over again, even if some time has passed.

One thing that can be helpful here is grounding. Grounding exercises are simple tools that bring you back to the present moment, helping to break the cycle of anxiety or flashbacks. Try focusing on something tangible, like the feel of a soft blanket or the sound of music. If you find yourself feeling overwhelmed, taking slow, deep breaths and naming a few things you can see, hear, or feel in that moment can help pull you back to the present. It's like telling your mind, *"I'm here, I'm safe, and I can handle this."*

Remember, having anxiety or PTSD-like symptoms after a loss doesn't mean something's wrong with you—it's simply a response to the intense emotions and memories connected to your pet. If these feelings start to interfere with your daily life or make it difficult to enjoy things, that's a sign that you might benefit from additional support. Taking care of yourself means acknowledging when these emotions become too much to handle alone, and there's no shame in seeking help to find some relief.

Each of these reactions is a reminder that our love for our pets is profound and deeply rooted in our lives. Whether it's recognizing signs of depression or facing unexpected waves of anxiety, know that you're not alone, and that support is out there, ready to help you through.

c. When to Seek Professional Help

Sometimes, despite our best efforts to cope, grief digs in deep, becoming a weight that's hard to carry alone. You may find that no amount of self-care, support from friends, or quiet reflection is helping you feel like yourself again. This is where professional help can come in, offering a safe space to talk through those feelings with someone who knows how to guide you through them. Seeking help doesn't mean you're failing to cope; it means you're giving yourself the support you deserve.

Talking to a therapist, counselor, or grief specialist can feel intimidating at first—after all, opening up about such a personal loss to someone you don't know can feel daunting. But consider therapy like having a compassionate guide on this path. A therapist's role is to listen without judgment, to help you make sense of the complex feelings that come with loss, and to provide tools to navigate grief in a way that feels manageable. They're there to support you, helping to unpack whatever emotions are weighing you down.

One of the beautiful things about therapy is that it's tailored to you. Maybe you just need a few sessions to process specific memories, or perhaps ongoing support feels more helpful. Some therapists specialize in pet loss, understanding the unique bond between humans and animals, while others are general grief counselors who can help with any type of loss. Think of therapy as a custom-fit resource, designed to help you in a way that feels right for you.

It's also okay if you're not quite sure whether you "need" therapy. Sometimes, just knowing there's a safe space to talk can be a relief. You don't have to wait until you're at a breaking point to reach out—sometimes, talking things over before they become overwhelming is the best thing you can do for yourself. Therapy isn't about fixing you or making the grief disappear; it's about giving you a place to be heard, to reflect, and to find comfort in ways that feel genuine.

If you're considering therapy, there are several options to explore. Some people prefer one-on-one sessions, where they can build a connection with a therapist over time. Others might feel more comfortable in a group setting, where they can hear from others who have experienced similar losses. There are even online therapy options, which can be convenient if in-person sessions don't feel accessible or comfortable right now. The key is finding a setting that feels safe and supportive.

Reaching out for professional help is an act of self-care, a way of honoring the love and connection you had with your pet. It's acknowledging that this loss matters deeply and that you're allowed to need support as you navigate it. Just like you would care for a physical injury, caring for your heart and mind during this time is important. Grief doesn't have a timeline or a set of rules; it's simply a process that, with a bit of guidance, can lead you toward a place of healing.

Key Takeaways

When grief becomes overwhelming, or when sadness, anxiety, or even PTSD-like symptoms start affecting your daily life, it's a sign that more support might be needed. Recognizing these feelings isn't about labeling them as "good" or "bad," but about understanding how grief has impacted you and taking steps to care for yourself.

Recognizing signs of depression—such as persistent sadness, loss of interest, or a feeling of numbness—can help you see when grief may have evolved into something heavier. Giving yourself permission to acknowledge these feelings is the first step toward healing, whether that means practicing gentle self-care or reaching out for extra support.

Anxiety and PTSD after pet loss are common responses, especially after a traumatic loss. Symptoms may include intense memories, flashbacks, or a constant feeling of unease. Grounding techniques and self-compassion can help, but sometimes, these symptoms may require additional guidance from a therapist.

Seeking professional help is an act of self-love, a way to honor the bond you shared with your pet by allowing yourself to process this loss fully. Therapy offers a safe space to explore your feelings, find relief, and learn coping tools, reminding you that you don't have to face grief alone.

Ultimately, your journey through grief is a deeply personal one, and there's no "wrong" way to go about it. With understanding, self-compassion, and the right support, healing becomes a path you walk at your own pace, with each step bringing you closer to peace.

Chapter 13

Pets in the Afterlife: Spiritual Perspectives

a. Cultural and Religious Views on Animal Afterlife

Let's start with a question we've all wondered about at some point: if there's an afterlife, will our pets be there waiting for us? I mean, it wouldn't be much of a paradise if we couldn't have our furry (or scaly, or feathery) friends by our side, right? In fact, I'm convinced that whatever heaven looks like, it has a lot of room for pet beds, cat trees, and endless fields of chew toys.

Across cultures and religions, there are so many fascinating beliefs about animals in the afterlife. Take the "Rainbow Bridge" concept, for instance. If you've ever lost a pet, chances are someone's told you about this magical bridge where animals go after they pass. It's like a grand reunion spot where pets wait for their humans to join them one day. The thought of our pets crossing that bridge and hanging out in a pet paradise waiting for us is oddly comforting. Imagine your dog sprawled out on a cloud, living their best lazy life, or your cat perched in some heavenly meadow, still giving that same smug, "I own this place" look they had on Earth.

Then, there's the concept of reincarnation in Hinduism. According to this belief, our souls (and that includes animals!) are on a continuous journey through different lives. Some people even believe that a pet could come back in another form, even as another pet in our lives. Imagine your cat showing up as the next kitten you adopt, with the same sass and love of knocking things off the counter. Or your dog is coming back as the neighbor's pup, barking to say, "Hey! Remember me?"

Buddhism has a slightly different take, but it still sees animals as part of a continuous cycle of life. Some Buddhists believe that animals and humans are all part of the same web of existence, which means they share the same potential for spiritual evolution. It's comforting to think that your pet is on their own spiritual journey, perhaps advancing in the universe in ways we can only imagine.

In Christianity, views vary, but many people hold onto the hope that their pets will join them in heaven. Pope Francis even hinted that animals could have a place in the afterlife, which sparked all kinds of excited conversations about heaven's possible dog park. I can just imagine the gates of heaven, with St. Peter holding a treat and saying, *"Good boy! Come on in!"*

These beliefs all reflect a deep respect and love for animals, showing that, across cultures, we want to believe that the love we have for our pets continues beyond this life. Whether it's through the Rainbow Bridge, reincarnation, or a place in heaven, people have found meaningful ways to keep their pets close, even in spirit. I hope that I get to go to the Rainbow Bridge too.

b. Near-Death Experiences and Pet Visitations

Now, here's something that might give you a bit of comfort—and maybe some little goosebumps, too. Some people who've had near-death experiences (NDEs) say they saw their pets on the "other side." Imagine that: you're floating in this peaceful, bright place, and who's waiting for you? Your dog, sitting there wagging his tail, or your cat giving you that *"what the heck took you so long?"* look.

Stories about NDEs often include encounters with loved ones, and for many, that includes pets. People describe their pets as looking healthy and happy, as if they're saying, *"Don't worry, I'm good, and I'll see you when you're ready."* It's kind of wonderful to think that, in those moments between life and death, the ones who brought us so much love in life are there to offer peace and comfort.

Of course, these are deeply personal stories, and they don't follow any strict rules. Some people see their pets as clearly as if they were right there, while others feel a presence or just "know" their pets are nearby. Either way, the takeaway is that these encounters often bring a sense of peace to those who experience them.

And who's to say it's not real? Think about it: pets are experts in sensing our emotions, understanding us in ways that sometimes even other humans don't. Maybe they're attuned to us in ways that transcend this life. When someone recounts an NDE and says they saw their dog or cat, it's hard not to believe there's something very real to that connection.

For those of us still here, these stories can be a source of comfort. They remind us that, even if we don't have all the answers, love is a bond that doesn't seem to fade, even when life ends. Whether it's a dog waiting by the proverbial "gates" or a cat lounging in a sunbeam of the afterlife, these stories let us imagine that our pets are still there, keeping an eye out for us. And honestly, if there's anything waiting on the other side, I'd be thrilled if it included a tail wag or two.

The idea that our pets continue to exist in some form—whether as a memory, a spirit, or beliefs of the Rainbow Bridge—it offers a comforting reminder that love never truly fades. These stories, beliefs, and cultural perspectives help us find solace in the thought that those we love remain with us in some way, showing that the bond doesn't simply vanish.

c. Finding Comfort in Spiritual Beliefs

Whether or not we have concrete answers about the afterlife, many of us find comfort in believing our pets are somehow still with us.

Maybe it's a quiet moment when we feel their presence, or maybe it's in those dreams where they visit, clear as day as if they're just stopping by to say, *"Hey, I'm still here."* It's like they leave these gentle reminders, letting us know that their spirit hasn't drifted too far.

For some people, talking to their pets after they're gone is completely natural. It might sound a little unusual to an outsider, but to those who've loved and lost a pet, it feels as normal as breathing. There's something deeply comforting about saying "good morning" to their photo or whispering a quick "I miss you" as if they can still hear us. And who's to say they can't? If it brings you peace and eases the ache just a little, then why not?

Others find comfort in rituals or personal practices. Lighting a candle in their memory, creating a small space with their favorite toy or collar, or even just holding onto the blanket they used to curl up on—these little acts create a connection, a bridge that keeps their memory close. It's not about holding onto the pain but rather finding ways to keep their love as a part of your daily life. After all, they're woven into the fabric of who we are; it makes sense that we'd want to keep that connection alive.

Some people turn to meditation or prayer, finding a quiet place to reflect and feel close to their pet. A few moments of stillness, where you can close your eyes and remember them as if they were right beside you, can be incredibly healing. It's like tapping into the quiet presence they brought to our lives, a reminder that their spirit is with us, even if we can't see them. In those moments, you might even find yourself smiling, remembering the way they looked at you or the sound of their paws on the floor.

Then there are the signs—those little things that happen that make you stop and wonder if they're somehow sending you a message. Maybe you find a broken pet tag on a walk, or you hear a dog bark that sounds EXACTLY like you did, or hear a song that reminds you of them just when you need it most. Some people swear their pets "visit" in these little ways as if they're popping in to remind us they're still around. It might sound a bit whimsical, but sometimes those small signs are exactly what we need to feel connected to them.

Of course, everyone's beliefs are different, and that's the beauty of this journey. Spirituality isn't the same for everyone; it's a deeply personal path, unique to each person and each pet. The way you choose to honor your pet's spirit, the rituals or practices that bring you comfort—these are entirely your own. There's no right or wrong way to grieve, just like there's no rulebook for how to love.

In the end, maybe it doesn't matter if we know for certain what happens after our pets pass. What matters is the love that remains, the bond that feels just as real, even if they're no longer physically here. That love is the bridge, the invisible thread that keeps us connected, no matter where we are. Finding comfort in spiritual beliefs, whether big or small, traditional or personal, is simply about keeping that love close.

Key Takeaways

Navigating the loss of a pet often leads us to wonder about what comes next, and exploring spiritual perspectives can bring comfort in meaningful ways. Across cultures and beliefs, the hope that our pets are still with us—in spirit, memory, or even the afterlife—provides a sense of peace.

Cultural and religious views offer diverse perspectives on animal afterlife, from the Rainbow Bridge to reincarnation. These beliefs remind us that love for animals is universal and that many cultures find ways to honor and remember pets beyond this life.

Near-death experiences and pet visitations provide personal glimpses of what might lie beyond. Stories of people seeing their pets on "the other side" can bring comfort, making us feel that our furry friends are just waiting for us in some peaceful place, tails wagging, purrs humming.

Finding comfort in spiritual beliefs is a personal journey. Whether through quiet rituals, meditative moments, or simply feeling their presence in little signs, honoring your pet's spirit is about keeping their memory alive in ways that bring peace to your heart.

Ultimately, the love we have for our pets doesn't end when they pass. It continues in any way you want it to continue.

Chapter 14

The Science of Grief

a. Neurological Changes During Grief

Let's talk about grief and the brain. You might think of grief as something that just makes you sad, but it turns out it also has a bit of a field day with your brain. And by "field day," I mean it really goes to town, making it hard to focus, remember things, or even get out of bed some mornings. Losing a pet doesn't just tug at your heartstrings; it's like your brain decides to go through a major software update that you didn't ask for.

When we lose a pet, the areas of our brain responsible for emotion and attachment light up like a Christmas tree. Your brain has been wired for connection and companionship, so when that connection suddenly disappears, the brain needs time to adjust. It's almost as if your brain goes, *"Wait, where's my buddy? They should be here."* This can lead to that foggy feeling where simple tasks seem confusing, and your attention span feels like it's been through a funhouse maze—twisted, dizzy, and completely lost.

If you're wondering why your brain is so affected, it's because pets hold a special place in it. They bring us comfort, companionship, and a sense of routine. Losing them disrupts all of those things, and the brain, bless its heart, doesn't adapt overnight. Your neural pathways—the little highways that carry signals around your brain—were used to firing off happy connections every time your pet trotted over for a cuddle or gave you that *"I'm so glad you're here"* look. Without those moments, the brain has to rewire, which can make everything feel... off.

So, if you're feeling distracted or like you're moving in slow motion, it's not just you—it's your brain processing the loss. It's actually a sign of how deeply you were connected to your pet. These changes are temporary, though. Your brain is remarkable at adapting, and with time, it starts creating new pathways that will help you feel a bit more like yourself again.

b. The Chemistry of Loss: How Grief Affects Your Body

Now, let's talk about the body. You'd think grief would just stay in the heart or the mind, but nope—it decides to take a full tour. Losing a pet can actually impact your entire body, turning things like sleep, appetite, and energy levels completely upside down. Imagine grief as that uninvited guest who messes with everything in your house: it gets into your sleep schedule, messes with your eating habits, and gives you those random aches and pains.

This happens because grief affects our stress hormones, specifically cortisol. When you're grieving, your body pumps out cortisol as if it's preparing you to face a threat. Your body doesn't know the difference between physical danger and emotional pain—it just knows you're going through something intense, so it jumps into "fight or flight" mode. But instead of helping you fight off a bear or run from a saber-toothed tiger, it's just making you feel wiped out, tense, or on edge for no obvious reason.

So, if you're feeling a strange combination of exhaustion and restlessness, that's the grief hormone cocktail at work. You may feel tightness in your chest, get headaches, or even have stomach troubles. Basically, grief doesn't just play mind games—it throws your whole body into a loop, too. It's like your body just ran a marathon, even though all you did was sit and think about your pet.

Knowing this can be oddly comforting. These physical symptoms are normal responses to loss, a sign that your body is processing everything. Sometimes, just acknowledging, *"Oh, this is my body reacting to grief,"* can help you be more patient with yourself. It's your body's way of saying, *"I know you're going through something tough, so I'm here, reacting in my own way."*

Key Takeaways

Grief has a real impact on both mind and body, but understanding the science behind it can offer comfort and practical ways to cope. When we lose a pet, our brains and bodies undergo changes, responding to the emotional shock in ways that can feel overwhelming. Recognizing these reactions as part of the grieving process is a reminder of how deeply connected we are to our pets.

Neurological changes during grief can make everything feel a bit foggy as the brain adjusts to the loss of a loved one. This is a natural part of the process, showing us that our connection to our pets is wired deeply into our minds.

The body, too, responds to grief, often with physical symptoms triggered by stress hormones. By acknowledging these reactions, you can approach grief with a sense of patience and compassion, allowing yourself the time you need to heal.

Ultimately, grief is a journey, and the path is different for everyone. Understanding the science behind it gives you the grace to feel each emotion, honoring your pet's memory by caring for yourself. Healing becomes possible through small, intentional steps—one day, one breath, one memory at a time.

Chapter 15

Pet Loss in Special Circumstances

a. When a Pet Goes Missing

Losing a pet is always hard, but it's a completely different kind of heartbreak when a pet goes missing. It's like your heart went for a walk and forgot to return. One minute they're there, wagging their tail or curled up in their favorite spot, and the next, you're standing at the door, looking out into the empty space, hoping for a familiar face to appear. The silence feels deafening, and every creak of the house or rustle outside makes you jump, praying that it's them returning home. The uncertainty is unbearable, leaving you with a constant ache, wondering where they are, if they're safe if they're hurt. Are they hungry? Are they cold? Are they trapped and can't get out of somewhere? And my worst feeling is that they are wondering why I haven't come to get them yet. It's a mix of helplessness, fear, and a deep longing that doesn't fade with time. You can't help but replay every moment with them, wishing you could have done something differently, anything to keep them from leaving that day.

The emotional rollercoaster of a missing pet is its own brand of chaos. You start off with panic, pacing the house while calling their name like you're summoning a genie. Then comes the adrenaline-fueled search, shaking a bag of treats at 3 a.m. outside in your housecoat and slippers, hoping they'll come trotting back with that "Geez, what's all the fuss about?" look.

Let's be real: it's exhausting. You're part detective, part emotional wreck, and part marathon runner, all while clinging to hope. You're checking lost pet websites, creating posters, and talking to neighbors as if you've suddenly become the local spokesperson for Missing

Pets Anonymous. It's a full-time job, fueled by love and caffeine (mostly caffeine).

Luckily, feeling all over the place is normal. When a pet goes missing, your brain goes into overdrive, flipping between "They're fine; they'll be back any second" and "What if they're stuck somewhere?" It's like living in a horror movie, where every noise outside is dramatic enough to make your heart leap. You're not just grieving; you're waiting. And this type of waiting, as you've probably noticed, this type of waiting is the emotional equivalent of staring at your phone while it charges to 99% but suddenly drops back to 1%.

So, how do you cope with the uncertainty? Start by doing what you can, even if it feels small. Post those flyers. Knock on doors. Reach out to local shelters and rescue groups. It might feel repetitive, but every action you take is a step toward finding them. And let's not underestimate the power of social media. A single post in a local group can reach hundreds of eyes—and one of those eyes might spot your furry escape artist.

While you're searching, permit yourself to take breaks. Yes, I know—how can you rest when your pet is out there? Running on empty doesn't help anyone, least of all you. Make time to eat, hydrate, and sit down for a moment. Even Sherlock Holmes had to pause for tea, and you're basically in detective mode right now.

And let's talk about hope. Hope can feel heavy, like carrying a balloon that's slowly deflating. Some days, it's hard to hold onto. That's okay. Hope isn't about pretending everything's fine; it's about believing in possibilities. Maybe your pet is exploring, safe, and curious, or maybe someone kind has taken them in. Let yourself imagine those good outcomes—they're not promises, but they're not impossibilities, either.

Finally, lean on others. Whether it's friends, family, or online pet communities, there's no shame in asking for help. People genuinely want to support you, whether it's sharing your post, helping with the search, or just listening to you vent about how you wish your pet had mastered the art of basic navigation and could find its way home like a well-behaved GPS with fur, instead of treating every detour like a thrilling adventure in a maze of poor decisions.

If you believe in psychics, perhaps consider visiting one. They might offer you insight that brings the closure you're seeking.

When a pet goes missing, it's a unique kind of heartbreak, one that comes with its own blend of hope, worry, and love. And through it all, remember this: the love you feel is what drives you to search, to hope, and to keep going. That love is a powerful thing, and no matter the outcome, it's a testament to the bond you share—a bond that's stronger than any distance. Don't give up.

b. Coping with Traumatic or Sudden Loss

Losing a pet is always tough, but when it's sudden or traumatic, it feels like someone yanked the rug out from under your feet while you were balancing a stack of emotions. One minute, they're there— bringing joy, companionship, and usually a little chaos—and the next, they're gone. There's no warning, no soft landing. It's like an emotional car crash, leaving you stunned and scrambling to understand what just hit you.

The shock of sudden loss probably hits you harder than you'd expect. You might feel numb, like the world has dimmed and everything is moving in slow motion. Or maybe you're overwhelmed by waves of emotions that don't seem to follow any logical order. Sadness, guilt, anger—they all crash into each other like bumper cars, leaving you feeling broken, exhausted, and unsure of what to feel next. And let's not forget the endless *what-ifs*. *What if I'd noticed something sooner? What if I had just double-checked the gate lock?* It's as if your brain becomes a 24/7 rerun of all the things you wish you had done.

Traumatic loss has a way of pulling every emotion to the surface, even ones you didn't know you had. It's your mind and body trying to process something that doesn't feel real yet. Give yourself permission to feel all of it—the sadness, the anger, even the guilt.

One of the hardest parts of sudden loss is the lack of closure. When you don't have time to say goodbye or prepare for the loss, it can leave you with a lingering sense of "unfinished business." Maybe you wish you'd given them one last treat, one more belly rub, or just a little extra time. It's okay to mourn those missed moments— they're a reflection of how much you cared. But try to remind yourself that the love you gave while they were here mattered far more than any single goodbye could.

If you're struggling to process the trauma, talking about it can help, too. Whether it's with a friend, family member, or a therapist, saying the words out loud can make the weight feel a little lighter. Again, share the memories with them, the funny stories, even the details of what happened if you feel ready. Sometimes, just having someone listen—really listen—can bring a sense of comfort and understanding.

Journaling can also be a powerful tool for coping. Write about your favorite memories, the quirks that made your pet unique, and even the painful parts of their loss. Think of it as having a conversation with them, a way to keep their presence alive in your heart. You don't have to be a poet or a novelist; just let the words flow, whether they're messy, raw, or even incomplete..

One more thing: if the loss feels too overwhelming to bear, don't hesitate to seek professional help. A grief counselor or therapist can provide a safe space to unpack those emotions and guide you through the healing process. Reaching out for help isn't a sign of weakness—it's a way of honoring the bond you shared by taking care of yourself.

Traumatic loss is never easy, and there's no way to make it painless. But through the tears, the anger, and the heartbreak, there's one constant: the love you shared. That love doesn't disappear just because they're gone. It stays with you, woven into the fabric of who you are, a reminder that their presence in your life matters. Healing doesn't mean forgetting—it means learning to carry that love in a new way, even as you move forward.

Above all, be gentle with yourself. Grief is messy, unpredictable, and often overwhelming, but it's also a reflection of how deeply you care. Allow yourself the time and space to heal, knowing that it's okay to feel broken for a while. And when the pain feels too heavy, remind yourself that you gave them a life full of love, and that love will always be enough.

c. Grieving a Pet You Had to Rehome

Let's start with a big, comforting truth: rehoming a pet is one of the most selfless and heartbreaking acts of love you can make. It's not an easy choice, and it often leaves you feeling like your heart has been pulled in two directions—grieving their absence while knowing you did what was best for them. It's like writing a breakup letter to someone you still love, except this "someone" doesn't understand the words; they just know you're not there anymore.

Rehoming a pet often comes with a heavy dose of guilt. Maybe it was a life change—moving, health issues, or financial struggles—or maybe it was about your pet's specific needs, ones you couldn't meet but someone else could. Whatever the reason, it's easy to get caught in the endless loop of *"Was there another way?"* or *"Did I fail them?"* But here's the thing: making a decision that prioritizes their well-being, even when it breaks your heart, is not failure. It's love in its purest, most painful form.

That doesn't mean it's easy, though. The grief of rehoming a pet is unique. Unlike losing a pet to illness or old age, rehoming carries a kind of bittersweet ache. On one hand, you know they're alive and hopefully thriving in their new home. On the other, you miss them like crazy and wonder if they miss you too. It's a tug-of-war between relief and longing, hope and heartache.

If you find yourself consumed by guilt, try to reframe the situation. Think about the reasons you made this decision and remind yourself of the love that guided it. Maybe their new home has a big backyard to run in, or maybe they're getting the undivided attention they need. Imagine them happy, cared for, and safe. It doesn't erase the pain, but it can help soften the edges, reminding you that this was about their happiness, not your comfort.

It's also okay to grieve their absence in the same way you would any other loss. You might still glance at their favorite spot on the couch, instinctively reach for their leash, or hear phantom barks or meows in the quiet moments. Those habits don't disappear overnight, and neither does the love you feel for them. Allow yourself to feel the loss without judgment. Missing them doesn't mean you made the wrong choice—it means they left a paw print on your heart that time won't erase.

If you have the opportunity, staying in touch with their new family can be incredibly healing. A photo or update about how they're settling in can bring a sense of peace, knowing they're loved and thriving. That said, not everyone has this option, and that's okay too. If updates feel too painful or aren't possible, focus on the memories you shared and the knowledge that you gave them the best start you could.

Most importantly, be kind to yourself. Rehoming a pet doesn't erase the love you had—or still have—for them. It's a choice rooted in care, not abandonment, and it takes immense courage to put their needs above your own heartbreak. Let yourself grieve, cry, and remember them fondly, knowing that your decision came from a place of selfless love.

In time, the pain of missing them may fade, leaving behind the happy memories of the life you shared. And even though they're not with you anymore, the love you gave them—and the love they gave you—will always remain. That love, as bittersweet as it feels now, is the greatest gift you could have given each other.

Chapter 16

The Workplace and Pet Loss

a. Asking for Time Off: Pet Bereavement Policies

Grief is strange—sometimes it hits you out of nowhere, like a ninja, and other times, you can see it coming from a mile away, like a bowling ball heading straight for your stomach. And when that grief involves the loss of a pet, you might find yourself in a situation where the last thing you want to do is put on your "professional" face and pretend you didn't just lose your best friend.

So, here you are, navigating the labyrinth of office emails, deadlines, and meetings, all while your heart feels like it's been dropped into a blender. If you've ever had to ask for time off due to the loss of a pet, you know it can feel like you're requesting permission to take a day off for something ridiculous—like "National Nap Day" or "Sock Appreciation Day." Pet loss isn't always seen as the "serious" kind of grief in the workplace, but let's be real: the loss of a pet is a heavy weight on your heart, and sometimes, you need a day (or a few) to process it.

So, what do you do? You take a deep breath and figure out how to navigate this with the same grace you pretend to have while answering emails about things you didn't understand (like that whole quarterly report thing). First, check your company's pet bereavement policy, if they have one. Yes, that's right—some workplaces actually offer time off for pet loss! If they do, it's your golden ticket to taking some time for yourself without feeling guilty. But if your company doesn't have an official policy (and sadly, not all do), don't be afraid to approach your boss or HR politely requesting a personal day.

It's all about framing it in a way that gets the message across: "I'm going through something deeply emotional, and while I might not have a human family member passing away, my pet was my family." Pet grief is real, and asking for time off doesn't make you a drama queen; it makes you human. If they need a little extra convincing, you can add that you'll be back refreshed and ready to tackle that mountain of emails. Except for the random bursts of uncontrollable sobbing when someone mentions a deadline.

b. Returning to Work After Pet Loss

So, you've taken some time off, you've shed your fair share of tears, and now it's time to return to work. Maybe you're dreading it—because, let's face it, how do you pretend everything is fine when you just want to go home, hug your pet's old favorite toy, and cry for another few weeks?

The idea of returning to your cubicle or your desk can feel like walking back into a room full of awkward conversations and uncomfortable silences. People might not know what to say, and let's be honest, some might not even realize how much your pet meant to you. You're probably bracing yourself for that one co-worker who, in their attempt to be supportive, gives you a pat on the back and says, "It's just a pet; you'll be fine." Cue the eye twitch.

But here's the thing—returning to work doesn't mean you need to put on a mask and pretend to be "over it." Grief is a process, and it doesn't follow any timeline or set of expectations. You can take your time, and it's okay if you're not all chipper the moment you clock back in. Maybe you don't feel like participating in that group meeting where everyone's talking about their weekend plans. Maybe you want to focus quietly on your tasks without the usual social distractions. That's totally fine.

What helps is acknowledging your grief in whatever way feels comfortable to you. If you're okay with it, you can simply say something like, "I'm going through a tough time after losing my pet, and I'm taking things one step at a time." You don't have to go into details if you're not ready, but just letting people know where you are emotionally can set the stage for understanding.

And don't be afraid to ask for what you need, whether it's adjusting your schedule or asking for a little more space when things feel overwhelming. Think of it like having a bad hair day, but on a much more emotional level. It's okay to not have it all together all the time.

c. Educating Colleagues About Pet Loss Grief

Not everyone understands that pet loss grief is real grief. For some, pets are "just animals," while for others, they're like family members, best friends, and personal therapists all rolled into one furry package. So, what do you do when you have to educate your colleagues about why you're not exactly in the mood for small talk or your usual Monday morning banter?

Start with a little humor. Lighten the mood with something like, "I know it might seem silly, but I'm grieving the loss of my four-legged friend who was basically my personal therapist—minus the hefty bill." A little humor can help set the tone and open the conversation in a way that isn't too heavy. After that, gently explain that pet loss can be just as emotionally impactful as losing a human loved one. You might even want to share how your pet was a constant presence in your life, offering unconditional love and comfort. It's important to give them context so they can understand the depth of your grief. For me, laughter got me through a lot of times when I wanted to burst into tears in public. Laughter might seem out of place, but it can be surprisingly helpful when you are trying to hold it all together during those tough moments.

It's also helpful to encourage your colleagues to be compassionate and patient. Let them know that you might need some space to process things or that you might not be your usual cheerful self for a while. Maybe offer suggestions for how they can support you, whether that's giving you a little extra time on a project or simply respecting your need for quiet.

It's not about making them feel guilty for not understanding, but rather helping them recognize that grief is not one-size-fits-all. Sometimes, people just need to be reminded that pets are family, too, and the pain of losing them can take time to heal.

And if all else fails, just remember: you don't have to carry the weight of the world alone, even at work. Sometimes, the best thing you can do is take a deep breath, ask for what you need, and trust that your coworkers—no matter how awkward they are about it— will come around.

Chapter 17

Helping Others Through Pet Loss

a. What to Say (and What Not to Say)

For me, when someone I care about loses a pet, the feeling of comforting them is so strong that I have to be very careful what I say because if it's the wrong thing, it can make them feel even worse. Speaking from experience.

First, let's talk about what **not** to say. As tempting as it might be to be the "optimistic friend," there are some phrases that sound more like a passive-aggressive pep talk than genuine comfort. I want to throat-punch anyone that says:

"They're just a pet." — Oof. This one is like telling someone, "Oh, your TV doesn't work anymore? Just buy a new one." For me and for most other people, pets are considered family, and downplaying their pain can feel dismissive and hurtful.

"At least it wasn't a human." — This might be intended to soften the situation, but it can easily feel dismissive of their pain. You wouldn't say that about someone's best friend, so why say it about your "best friend"?

"They're in a better place." — While well-meaning, this can be a bit too much, especially if the grieving person is still in the raw, painful phase. Sometimes, they just want to sit with the grief for a while. (and wouldn't the better place be here with you still?) Man, I hate that one.

Now, for the magic words—*what to say*. Start with the simplest but often most impactful statement:

"I'm so sorry for your loss." — Direct, compassionate, and to the point. It acknowledges their grief without over-explaining.

"I'm here for you." — Offer your presence, not just your sympathy. Let them know you're available to listen, cry with them, or just sit in silence.

"I can't imagine how hard this must be for you." — Empathy is powerful. Acknowledging the depth of their pain can make them feel understood without trying to offer a quick fix.

"What can I do to help?" — This is your best option if you're unsure what they need. It lets them guide the support, which can feel like a weight lifted when they don't have to figure it out alone.

Tip: If you're in doubt, the classic "I'm here for you" can never go wrong. Just be present and ready to listen without judgment. Sometimes, saying nothing at all is the most healing thing you can do. I also appreciate a hug. Nothing else. No words. Just a hug. But not in public because I would immediately start crying.

b. Practical Ways to Support a Grieving Pet Owner

So, you've figured out the right words to say (or not say), and now you're wondering, "What can I actually do to help my friend who's hurting?" Grief can leave people feeling isolated, so your job is to show them that they're not alone in this. But how do you do that without feeling like you're trying to give them a pep talk or take away their pain (spoiler alert: you can't take away their pain, but you can help carry it)?

Here are some practical ways to show up for someone who's grieving their pet:

1. Offer a Listening Ear

Sometimes, the best thing you can do is simply be there to listen. Let them share their favorite memories, their heartache, and the little things they miss about their pet. Don't try to fix it; just listen. It can be a huge comfort to let someone express their feelings without interruption or advice.

2. Cook a Meal or Order Takeout

Grief can make even the simplest tasks feel impossible. Take the weight off their shoulders by providing some nourishment. Whether it's dropping off a homemade casserole or ordering their favorite comfort food, this small act of kindness can go a long way in showing you care.

3. Help with the Practical Stuff

If they're too overwhelmed to handle basic tasks, offer to step in. Run errands, help with grocery shopping, or take care of their pets' things if they can't bring themselves to do it. It might feel awkward at first, but offering practical support lets them focus on healing rather than the everyday logistics.

4. Create a Memory Box or Scrapbook

If they're open to it, help them create a memory box filled with mementos of their pet—paw prints, favorite toys, or photos. It can be a beautiful way to honor their pet's memory and keep the love alive long after they're gone. The thoughtfulness of offering this can help your friend feel like they're not alone in remembering their pet's unique spirit.

5. Share Funny Pet Stories or Pictures

If your friend is in a place where they can smile, share a funny memory or a silly picture of their pet. It's like finding an unexpected little spark of joy in the middle of the darkness. Laughter can sometimes heal wounds in ways that sympathy alone can't.

c. Being There for the Long Haul

Grief is a marathon, not a sprint. And while the initial days and weeks after losing a pet can be filled with an outpouring of support, what often gets overlooked is that the pain doesn't just go away. The quiet moments, the anniversaries, and the random things that remind someone of their pet—they all bring up that same ache. So, if you want to be a friend who truly helps, showing up for the long haul is key.

Check in periodically. Not just in the first few days, but in the weeks and months that follow. Grief doesn't adhere to a schedule, and while your friends might seem okay one day, they may be struggling the next. A simple text or phone call that says, "Thinking of you today. How are you doing?" can be a lifeline when the grief feels isolating.

Also, keep in mind that their grief might not look like the dramatic, tear-filled breakdowns you saw in the beginning. Grief is a big mess, and it doesn't always show up as expected. Your friend may put on a brave face, or they may quietly retreat. The point is to keep offering support in ways that fit where they are emotionally.

Here's another thing to consider: they might not be ready to "move on" in the way others might expect. Do you know that one friend who insists that you need to "get over it" after a certain amount of time? Yeah, don't be that friend. Grief isn't a timeline, and no one can heal on a schedule. So, don't rush them. Instead, offer ongoing emotional support and patience.

After a significant loss, people need time to remember and process the love they shared. It's not always about cheering them up or offering solutions; sometimes, it's about being there for the long run. Grief doesn't just go away, and neither should you. By being there for them—even months after their pet has passed—you're letting them know that you care enough about them to be there for every step of their journey, no matter how long it may be. And being there for the long haul is also about staying consistent. And hey, if you ever need to offer your friend an extra box of tissues and a good laugh, consider it a small but important role you're playing in their healing journey. They will appreciate it more than you think.

Comforting others through pet loss is all about patience, kindness, and for me, offering a little bit of humor when the moment is right. It's your support of all of the above that makes a world of difference.

Chapter 18

Moving Forward: The Healing Journey

a. Recognizing Signs of Healing

In the previous chapter, we talked about how to support friends through their grief, and while being there for others is important, eventually, the focus has to shift back to your own healing. It's not a sprint, and there's no set number of days to "get over it"—but it's important to notice when healing starts to happen. These signs might appear slowly, like those rogue chin hairs, but eventually, you'll start spotting them more frequently.

1. You're Able to Smile at the Memories

One of the first signs of healing is when the memories of your pet start to bring more smiles than tears. The goofy photos, the sweet moments, and the way they made you laugh on your worst days start to feel more like joyful snapshots of the life you shared, rather than painful reminders of the void they left. It's like finding a buried treasure in a pile of sand—you can finally see the shine, even if it's been hidden for a while.

If you're starting to laugh about the ridiculous things your pet did— whether it was the way they quickly spun in circles when you asked them if they wanted to go for a walk, or their antics that used to drive you crazy but now, you think they are funny (and you actually miss them)—well, that's a pretty big sign you're healing. It's a healthy way of remembering them, where you don't just see the sadness but the life and joy they brought into your world. I remember that Lucy used to wake me up in the middle of the night sometimes for a belly rub! That drove me nuts! I used to get mad and say, "Lucy! You don't wake Mommy up for tummy rubs!"

Now, I can laugh at it.

2. The Thought of Them No Longer Brings Tears, But Gratitude

You might start to notice that when you think of your pet, there's a warm, fuzzy feeling of gratitude instead of the tears immediately following. The ache is still there but is accompanied by a deep appreciation for everything they gave you. The grief starts to soften into thankfulness for the love, companionship, and memories they left behind. It's like a switch in the soundtrack of your life, moving from the sad and heartbreaking songs from a "Journey" album to the CD that's played while you are getting a great massage. You know what I mean.

3. You Can Talk About Them Without Breaking Down

At some point, you may notice that you can speak about your pet without feeling your chin quiver or your eyes starting to fill with tears. You start saving money, not having to buy so much tissue paper. You're no longer locked in that fragile space where just mentioning their name brings that wave of tears. Instead, you may share their story with others, reminiscing about the good times, and yes, even the challenges they might have presented (because let's be real, pets aren't perfect). That's a sign of growth—it means you've moved from just surviving their loss to beginning to live with it, integrating it into your story.

4. You Feel a Sense of Peace When You Remember Them

This is when the fog of grief starts to lift, and you feel at peace with their memory. It's not about forgetting, but more about accepting that they will always be part of your life, even if they're no longer physically here. You may not always be sad when you think of them; instead, you'll feel a quiet comfort, like that nostalgic smell of moth balls that reminds you of your late Great Grandmother.

As we discussed, healing doesn't happen all at once, and it's not about forgetting the pain. It's about learning how to carry their memories, and even the grief in a way that no longer keeps you feeling like you are stuck in a mud hole. Just because you start to heal doesn't mean you've forgotten. It means you've found a way to get out of the mud and move forward while honoring the past.

b. Integrating the Loss into Your Life Story

Recognizing healing is an important step, but the next part of the journey is learning to use their memory in your life story. Their presence shaped you—your routines, your heart, and even how you see the world. Moving forward doesn't mean erasing that chapter; it means understanding how it continues to influence the story of *you*.

1. Acknowledge Their Role in Your Life

Every pet, whether they were with you for 20 years or 20 weeks, leaves a mark. They might have taught you patience (*like house training taking 8 months!*), made you laugh during tough moments (*like farting in their sleep while you are breaking up with your boyfriend*), or simply have just been a steady companion when you needed one the most. Reflect on how they changed your life. Maybe you're a more compassionate person because of them, or maybe they motivated you to get out of bed on those days when you just didn't want to. Maybe they were the only living beings that you ever felt really loved and needed you. These lessons don't disappear when they do—they stay with you, shaping the way you navigate the world.

Think of it this way: your pet was a character in your story, and even though their chapter has ended, their influence ripples through the pages that follow. Acknowledge how they've helped you grow, and let their legacy be part of the ongoing narrative.

2. Create Traditions to Honor Their Memory

Incorporating your pet's memory into your life doesn't have to be grand or complex. It can be as simple as wishing them a happy birthday on their birthday, revisiting their favorite spot on walks, or keeping a photo of them where you'll see it every day. These small acts are like keeping their spirit alive, reminding you of the joy and love they brought into your life.

Some people choose to create memorials, like planting a tree or dedicating a small space in their garden to their pet. Others might make donations to animal shelters or volunteer in their pet's honor. These gestures don't just honor your pet's memory—they also turn their loss into a source of positive energy that continues to impact the world.

3. Share Their Story with Others

If you're comfortable, sharing your experience of loss with others can also help. It not only honors your pet but also opens the door for conversations about grief and healing. You never know—your story might be exactly what someone else needs to hear as they navigate their own loss.

4. Carry Their Lessons Forward

Every pet had something to teach us, whether it was that unconditional love, that resilience, or their art of finding joy in the smallest things (like a crumpled ball of paper or a stick from the backyard). As you move forward, think about how you can carry those lessons with you. Maybe it's being more present with loved ones, showing kindness to others, or just taking time to relax and sprawl out in the sunshine, like your pet always did.

Integrating their loss into your life doesn't mean leaving them behind—it means allowing their memory to shape the person you're becoming. They may not be here physically, but their impact will be eternal.

c. Finding New Purpose After Pet Loss

Once you've recognized healing and started to integrate your pet's memory into your life story, you might find yourself asking, *"What's next?"* It's a big question, and one that can feel both exciting and overwhelming. Losing a pet can leave a gap in your life, but it also opens the door to new possibilities—new ways to honor their memory, find meaning, and rediscover purpose.

1. Channeling Grief Into Positive Action

Grief is powerful—it can feel like huge waves that keep knocking you down, but it also has the potential to fuel meaningful change. Many people find solace in turning their loss into something good, like volunteering at an animal shelter, fostering pets, or even starting a fundraiser for animal rescue organizations. It's like taking the love you have for your pet and letting it ripple outward, touching the lives of other animals who need care and compassion.

Even small actions can create a sense of purpose. Maybe you sponsor a shelter pet in honor of your furry friend or donate to a cause they would have "approved of" ('cause you know they would have had an opinion about this one). These acts aren't just about helping others—they're about keeping your pet's spirit alive in a way that feels tangible and impactful.

2. Opening Your Heart to New Connections

For some, the idea of welcoming a new pet feels impossible after a loss. *"How could I ever love another the way I loved them?"* is a question that many people wrestle with. But honestly, loving a new pet doesn't replace the one you lost—it's simply an extension of the love they taught you. It's like your heart grows a bit bigger so that you can love again without losing any of the space you've already filled for the ones you've loved before.

You might consider adopting or fostering a new pet when the time feels right (and only when it feels right). This isn't about "moving on"—it's about opening your heart to another soul who needs the kind of love you're so good at giving. And if you're not ready? That's okay, too. Purpose doesn't have to mean rushing into something new—it can be about waiting until the right connection comes along, and when it does, you will know.

3. Sharing Your Experience to Help Others

One of the most meaningful ways to find purpose after pet loss is by helping others navigate their own grief. Remember how overwhelming it felt when you were in the thick of it? Now, imagine being able to offer someone else a lifeline—a listening ear, a kind word, or even just the reassurance that they're not alone.

You don't have to be a grief counselor to make a difference. It could be as simple as supporting a friend who's just lost their pet, volunteering in a pet loss support group, or even writing about your experience like I have. Sharing your story not only helps others—it also reinforces your own healing, showing you how far you've come.

4. Finding Joy in New Routines

Losing a pet often leaves a hole in your daily routine. No more walks, no more mealtime rituals, no more snuggles on the couch. At first, this emptiness can feel unbearable, like your day has lost its rhythm. But over time, finding new routines can be a way to reclaim your sense of balance.

Maybe you take up a new hobby—gardening, painting, or even learning to draw. Perhaps you pour energy into your relationships with family, friends, or even other animals in your life. These new routines don't erase what you've lost, but they give your days new meaning, helping you find joy in small, unexpected places.

5. Reflecting on What They Taught You

Every pet brings something unique to our lives, and part of finding purpose after their loss is reflecting on the lessons they left behind. Did they teach you patience? Resilience? The value of a good nap in front of a roaring fire? Carry those lessons forward, letting them guide you as you move into this new chapter.

Think of it this way: your pet may no longer be here physically, but their legacy lives on in the way you live your life. Every act of kindness, every moment of joy, and every bit of love you give is a tribute to the bond you shared. That's the purpose in its purest form—living in a way that honors the life they helped you create.

6. Embracing the New Chapter

Moving forward after a pet loss doesn't mean leaving them behind—it means carrying their memory with you as you step into a new chapter. It's about finding ways to turn the love and lessons they gave you into something meaningful, whether that's through helping others, creating new connections, or simply living with more intention.

This chapter of your life may feel unfamiliar, but it's also full of possibilities. By allowing yourself to grow, to love again, and to find purpose in the wake of loss, you're not just healing—you're honoring the love that started it all. Your pet's story doesn't end with their passing. It lives on in the way you carry their memory and let it shape the person you're becoming.

Take this new chapter one step at a time. The journey forward may be different, but it's yours to shape, guided by the love that will always remain.

Chapter 19

To Love Again: Welcoming a New Pet

a. How to Know When (or If) You're Ready

Here we are, at the final stretch of this journey—a path that's taken us through heartbreak, healing, and rediscovering purpose. If you've made it this far, you've already done the hard work of acknowledging your grief and finding ways to honor your pet's memory. But now, a new question might be tiptoeing into your mind: *Am I ready to love another pet?*

First things first—there's no timeline to welcome a new companion into your life. For some, the idea of adopting again feels unthinkable for months or even years. For others, the silence left behind by their pet is unbearable, and the thought of bringing in a new soul feels like the best way to heal. Both are valid, and both come with their own set of emotions.

1. Listening to Your Heart

One of the best indicators that you might be ready is when the idea of loving another pet starts to feel exciting instead of daunting. It's not about "replacing" your previous pet—after all, they were one of a kind—but about opening your heart to a new kind of connection. If you find yourself smiling at adoption ads or daydreaming about walks in the park, that might be your heart's way of saying it's ready to try again.

But let's be honest, readiness isn't always a lightning-bolt moment. Sometimes, it's more of a hesitant curiosity, like dipping your toes into cold water. You might not feel 100% sure, and that's okay. Love often grows in the unexpected moments, not in the perfectly planned ones.

2. Checking In With Yourself

Ask yourself some honest questions:

Do I feel ready to commit to the care and responsibility of another pet?

Am I looking for a new pet to fill a void, or am I ready to embrace them as their own unique being?

Do I have the time, energy, and resources to provide a good home right now?

If your answers lean toward readiness, that's a good sign. But if you feel unsure or hesitant, give yourself more time. Remember, there's no rush. The right moment will come when it's meant to.

3.Understanding That Grief and Love Can Coexist

One of the biggest hurdles for many is the feeling of guilt. *If I get a new pet, does it mean I'm moving on?* Absolutely not. Welcoming a new pet doesn't erase your love for the one you lost—it's simply a way to let your heart grow. Think of it like planting a new tree in a garden that already has beautiful flowers. The new tree doesn't replace the flowers; it simply adds more beauty to the space.

Recognizing When You're Not Ready

On the flip side, if the thought of a new pet brings up more anxiety than excitement, that's a sign to wait. Grief is unpredictable, and forcing yourself into something you're not ready for can make the process harder. Trust your instincts—they're usually right.

Letting the Idea Bloom Naturally

Sometimes, the best things happen when you're not actively looking. A friend might mention a litter of kittens, or you might stumble upon an adoption event and feel that inexplicable tug toward one particular furry face. You'll know when the timing is right—not because someone tells you, but because your heart whispers, *"It's time."*

In the end, the decision to love again is deeply personal. It's not about rushing into something because you feel you should—it's about honoring your heart's journey and listening when it says, *"I'm ready to open up again."*

b. Honoring Your Past Pet While Loving a New One

Bringing a new pet into your life is a beautiful act of hope and love, but let's not pretend it's without its emotional complications. You've spent this journey honoring your past pet, carrying their memory forward, and now, the thought of loving another can feel bittersweet. How do you make space in your heart for a new companion without feeling like you're leaving your old friend behind?

Here's the secret: your heart isn't a suitcase with limited room—it's more like a house with infinite rooms. Loving a new pet doesn't mean closing the door on your past one; it means opening a new door while keeping all the other ones wide open.

1. Acknowledge That Each Pet Is Unique

Your previous pet was one of a kind. Like if they would go down the carpeted stairs to the basement and slide down on their belly like it was a slide, or how they would try to bite the windshield wipers as they were going back and forth in the car. Whatever quirks made them special, they're irreplaceable. That doesn't mean there isn't room for another unique soul with their own quirks to join your life. Your new pet won't be a carbon copy, and they're not meant to be. They'll bring something entirely new to the table—and that's part of the beauty.

2. Keep Their Memory Alive

Some people find it meaningful to incorporate their past pet into their new pet's life. For instance, maybe your new dog wears the same winter coat or uses the same leash. Or you pass down that cozy bed that still holds the essence of your old companion. These little acts can feel like you're weaving their stories together, creating a sense of continuity between the old and the new.

3. Be Kind to Yourself About Comparisons

It's natural to compare your new pet to your old one—especially in the early days. You might find yourself thinking, *"They don't cuddle the same way,"* or *"Why don't they understand me like my old dog did?"* This is completely normal. Remember, your bond with your past pet was built over time, not overnight. Give your new pet the same patience, love, and trust that a unique bond will grow in its own way.

When comparisons sneak in, try to reframe them. Instead of thinking, *"They'll never be like my old cat,"* shift it to, *"They're teaching me a whole new way to love."* It's not about erasing the past; it's about expanding your capacity to love.

4. Let Both Pets Shape You

Your past pet shaped you in ways you might not even realize—your patience, your joy, your understanding of unconditional love. And now, your new pet will continue that journey, adding their own lessons to the mix. Together, they'll leave a legacy that's uniquely yours, a blend of all the love and growth they brought into your life.

5. Embrace the New Chapter While Honoring the Old

Think of your life as a book, with each pet contributing a chapter. Your old pet's chapter is one you'll reread often, full of laughter, love, and unforgettable moments. Your new pet's chapter is still blank, waiting to be filled with its own set of memories. Loving them both isn't about closing one chapter and starting another—it's about adding to the story.

6. Find Joy in the Present

When your new pet does something funny or endearing, allow yourself to fully enjoy it. It's okay to laugh, to feel happy, and to love them deeply. These moments don't diminish your love for your past pet—they add to the richness of your life, reminding you that love is endless. It grows, adapts, and flourishes in ways you never thought possible.

In the end, honoring your past pet while loving a new one is about balance. It's about holding onto the love you shared while making space for new love to blossom. And it's about recognizing that your heart, vast and resilient, can carry them both without compromise.

c. The Adoption Process: Finding Your New Companion

Now that you've embraced the idea of opening your heart again and made peace with honoring your past pet, it's time to tackle the practical side of things: finding your new furry, feathered, or scaly companion. The adoption process can be exciting and overwhelming, and—let's be real—full of moments that make you question how anyone ever chooses just one. It's like when you were a kid, and your mom took you to a candy store and said you could pick one thing. Remember how hard that was? So ya, choosing just one perfect animal out of the 30 animals in the shelter seems impossible, right?

But don't worry—this part of the journey isn't about perfection. It's about connection. Here's how to approach it with an open heart and a clear mind.

1. 1. Reflect on What You're Looking For

Start by thinking about what kind of pet would fit your current lifestyle and needs. Are you ready for the boundless energy of a puppy that's peeing all over your house, or would a mellow senior dog that you can binge watch "Lost" with be a better match? Do you want a playful kitten who climbs everything in sight and hangs off your new curtains, or are you dreaming of a relaxed cat who will snuggle into your neck and rub its nose on your chin? Maybe you're considering a small pet like a rabbit or guinea pig, or even something unconventional, like a reptile.

As said earlier, this isn't about replacing your past pet—it's about finding a companion whose personality compliments yours right now. And remember, the perfect pet for you might not look anything like what you had in mind. Sometimes, it's the one you least expect that steals your heart.

2. **Do Your Homework**

It's time to research once you've narrowed down what you're looking for. Visit local shelters, rescue groups, or reputable breeders if you're looking for a specific breed. Many shelters have detailed profiles for their animals, including personality traits, energy levels, and any special needs. Reading these can help you find a match that feels right. You can also share details about your lifestyle with a shelter and the type of pet that would suit you, then ask them to reach out if one arrives that needs a loving home.

Also, don't forget to ask questions! If you're meeting a pet through a shelter or rescue, learn about their history, habits, and quirks. Are they good with kids or other animals? Do they have medical conditions you need to prepare for? The more you know, the better equipped you'll be to provide a loving home.

3. Trust the Connection

When you meet potential pets, pay attention to how you feel around them. Sometimes, the connection is immediate—a tail wag, a gentle purr, or even just a look that says, *"Hey, you're my person."* Other times, it takes a little longer. Either way, trust your instincts. The right companion will feel like a natural fit, even if they surprise you with traits or behaviors you didn't anticipate.

It's also okay if your first visit doesn't result in finding "the one." This isn't speed dating—it's about building a lifelong bond. Be patient, and let the process unfold in its own time.

4. Prepare Your Home

Before bringing your new pet home, make sure their space is ready. Gather the essentials: food, bedding, toys, leashes, collars, and any special items they might need. Will I need to put up a gate to keep them out of certain rooms? Will the family be home when we get there to have a slow and gentle introduction? Will I have time to just be with them once they are home?

If you're adopting from a shelter or rescue, ask if you can take home something that smells like their current environment, like a blanket or toy. This can help ease the transition and make them feel more secure in their new surroundings.

5. Embrace the Adjustment Period

Bringing a new pet home is exciting, but it's also an adjustment for both of you. Your new companion might be shy, curious, or even a little overwhelmed as they explore their new environment. Give them time to settle in and learn the routines of your household.

During this period, be patient and consistent. Set new routines for feeding, walks, and playtime, and use positive reinforcement to help them feel safe and loved. It's a learning curve for both of you, but those first few weeks are when the foundation of your bond is built. You may have to just leave them be until they are comfortable enough to approach you. Or maybe they need to be by your side constantly until they feel safe. Whatever it is that they need, allow them that adjustment time.

6. Celebrate the Journey

As you settle into life with your new pet, take time to celebrate the little moments. The first time they curl up next to you on the couch, their excitement when you come home, or even the way they make you laugh with their antics that you aren't used to—these are the memories that will fill the next chapter of your life.

7. Let Love Grow

The bond with your new pet won't replicate the one you had before, and it's not supposed to. It will be its own, unique relationship, built on the sweet moments, their funny quirks, and the love you will share together. Give it time, and let that love grow in its own way.

As you close this chapter and then this book, remember: welcoming a new pet isn't just about starting over—it's about continuing the journey of love and companionship that began with the pets who came before. Each pet leaves a pawprint on your heart, and each one helps prepare you for the next. The story doesn't end here—it keeps growing, one wag, one purr, or one precious moment at a time.

Thank you for taking the time to read my book. I hope that it gave you some sort of comfort, knowing that you aren't alone. I've been there too. It sucks, and at the beginning, I didn't think I was going to be able to pick myself up and move on, but eventually, my heart was ready and yours will be too.

Thank you for trusting that my book will help guide you through your grieving process. I'm truly honored to be a part of your journey, and I sincerely hope that I was able to provide you some comfort.

I'm so sorry for your loss,

Julie